"This book is full of healthy food for your mind and your soul. Whenever I follow this advice I'm a much happier person."

HARVEY MCKINNON, international award-winning film producer
and author of *Hidden Gold*

"More than a guide book, this is a profound and passionate testimony to the power of love and spiritual balance that can heal and transform our lives."

AZIM KHAMISA, award-winning author of
Azim's Bardo – A Father's Journey from Murder to Forgiveness and
founder and CEO of the Tariq Khamisa Foundation.

"Azim Jamal has created a recipe for long-term happiness with seven simple ingredients... a timely contribution as we enter the new millennium."

LEE-ANN MULROONEY, founder, directress, and
principal of Westside Montessori School, Vancouver, BC, Canada

---

This book examines the following:

- How do we navigate through the journey of life, enjoying the ride as well as reaching our destination?

- How can we happily meet the many challenges and obstacles we encounter on this journey, and at the same time be alert to the opportunities we meet along the way?

- How can we succeed and flourish while remaining true to our principles, ethics, and values?

- How can we reach our fullest potential and accomplish our mission in life?

- How can we be happy with whatever we have?

An *INSPIRING* *and* PRACTICAL

GUIDE *to* SUSTAINED HAPPINESS

7
SEVEN
STEPS *to*
LASTING
HAPPINESS

Azim Jamal

10151 Gilmore Crescent,
Richmond, BC V6X 1X1
Canada

Photography by Jonathan Cruz
Designed and printed by Bluestone Press Inc.
Printed in Canada.
First edition: July 1999
Reprinted: July 2000

Canadian Cataloguing in Publication Data
Jamal, Azim, 1955-
7 Steps to lasting happiness

Includes bibliographical references.
ISBN 0-9685367-0-0

1. Self-actualization (Psychology) I. Title II. Title: Seven
steps to lasting happiness

BF637.S4J35 1999   158:1   C99-910540-X

*I dedicate this book to my wife, Farzana, who has been by my side
and given me support and unwavering love;*

*my children, Sahar and Tawfiq, who are an inspiration and
the source of my energy;*

*my parents, Abdul and Shirin, who are my role models and whose
unconditional love has been a fountain of wisdom to me;*

*and, finally, my brothers, Mehboob and Shaffin, who have taught me
the meaning and value of diversity.*

The Seven Steps

CONTENTS

Acknowledgments

I gratefully acknowledge and express deep appreciation to the many wonderful people who assisted me in completing my book, including –

My wife, Farzana, for working side by side with me from the start of the project to the end; my mentors, Dad, Mum, Firoz Rasul, Harold Karro, Akber Ladha, Mohamed Manji, and Kamrudin Rashid, for their teachings in more ways than they can imagine; Patryce Kidd for doing the structural and substantive edit; Sharon Boglari for carrying out the copy edit and providing guidance; my friends Larry Kazdan, Sam Meisel, Khalil Shariff, Afzal Mangalji, and Salim Premji for their invaluable input throughout the progression of the book; Amin Jamal, for suggesting the title and other valuable feedback; Aly Lakhani, for guidance in the publishing process; Noordin Nanji, Nadir Mohamed, Dr. Saida Rasul, Nelin Ahamed, and Nurdin Dhanani for insightful input to the final draft; Malik Talib, Harvey McKinnon, Zainab Merali, Michael Lacusta, Azim Khamisa, Amyn Dahya, Alnoor Kassam, Naftali Ramrajskar, Alkarim Haji, Lee-Ann Mulrooney, Zulfikar Jiwa, Shehin Devji, Jack Whelan, Shabir Panjwani, Navin Virani, Ann Bon, Hanif and Shenaz Chatur, Peter Harnisch, Karim Hirji, Kabyr and Rozy Remtilla, Firoz Kheraj, Amir Kabani, Alkarim and Nimira Bapoo, Chris Ingvaldson, Almunir and Naz Remtulla, Rashida Tejani, Taj Mohamed, Shafik Keshavjee and Salima Alibhai for useful and practical feedback to my drafts; Bluestone Press for typesetting and printing the books; Working Design for designing the cover; Jonathan Cruz for taking the cover photograph; the many people other than those specifically mentioned above who provided valuable feedback to my earlier drafts; and my close friends, relatives, teachers, and sports associates who have played an important part in shaping this book.

To God whose grace and mercy has guided me every step of the way.

Thank you all.

Introduction

In the 1970s, I was studying in England. The proverbial poor student, I had no money and was living as frugally as possible – on many occasions sharing a small apartment with up to five other students. My staple food was the cereal Weetabix, which I ate morning, afternoon, and evening. It was cheap, healthy, and easy to prepare. Although I had friends, I had neither the time nor the income to do much socializing. In the summer, to pay my tuition costs, I worked by day cutting up dead chickens in a poultry factory, and by night washing clothes in a laundry.

Twenty years later, in the early 1990s, I found myself in considerably different circumstances. I was (and am still) married to a loving and wonderful wife and had two beautiful young children. My business practice was thriving, and I'd achieved a level of financial stability that my younger self would probably have envied. I was also a well-known and respected member of my community.

Certainly, I was happy. Yet, upon closer reflection, I had to admit I had been happier as a struggling student in England; material abundance had not given me more happiness. Looking at the many different people I knew and had known, I began to think about what made them truly happy – and what caused them sadness. This book is the product of years of questioning and reflection in my quest to find sustained happiness. I realized that lasting happiness comes from fully appreciating each waking moment, living with integrity and humility, striving to reach one's full potential, and making a difference in the lives of others. It is not based on what we have, but on what we are. It is something that is within us, not outside us. By following the seven steps to happiness outlined in this book, anyone who wants to do the rewarding work of improving his or her life and finding sustained happiness will benefit immensely.

The basic premise of my philosophy is that each one of us is born with a purpose – or mission – in life. Most of us ultimately ask much the same questions: What is my purpose in life? How will my performance in life be judged? How do I know if I am doing okay? What happens to me after I die? How do I best work toward my destiny?

Every person's mission is different. No two people in the universe are exactly the same, nor do they have the same experiences or upbringing. By keeping an open mind to our individual differences we can learn from others, and, through caring and sharing experiences, we can find happiness.

For happiness to be sustainable, it must involve all facets of our experience – from inner knowledge and attitudes to healthy relationships and spirituality. I have identified seven steps to lasting happiness, which I discuss in my book:

- Discover Yourself

- Maintain Positive Attitudes

- Hone Your Life Skills

- Build Healthy Relationships

- Let Ethics and Values Be Your Guide

- Awaken Your Spirituality

- Enjoy The Ride

The first step, "Discover Yourself," is perhaps the most difficult step to take, but it is the one from which all the others proceed. We need to know who we are and what we want before we can realize our true potential. As the process of self-discovery evolves, we change as well, and I suggest readers keep returning to this section in particular to clarify their missions. Although there is a logical progression through the steps from the physical platform to the spiritual, the steps are also overlapping, synergistic, and need not necessarily follow the sequence given in this book. For example, you do not have to work on step three, "Hone Your Life Skills" before working on step five, "Let Ethics and Values Be Your Guide."

Throughout the book, but particularly in the sixth section, "Awaken Your Spirituality," I address the topic of spirituality. I am in no way advocating a particular spiritual path; religious choices are entirely up to each individual. Yet it seems to me that all of us, regardless of differences in our particular religious beliefs, are inherently spiritual beings. Spirituality lies in the very act of living – and it doesn't matter what religious label we wear or if we are atheists or agnostics. A spiritual being is one who is connected to his or her spirituality irrespective of religious associations.

I also use examples that refer to a "traditional" family. This reflects my personal experience, but I realize that it might not echo that of all readers. Despite individual definitions of family, we share a common need for meaningful relationships. Everyone wants love, and everyone needs, for his or her own well-being, to love. Every successful relationship shares common traits of mutual respect and effective communication. So I am asking readers to look at the examples I give, not as prescriptive, but as illustrative of a universal human condition.

The principles in this book will be of little value if you do not translate them into action in your daily life. You need to implement and internalize them gradually. This is not something that can be done overnight; rather it is an ongoing process. I recommend that you read through the book once to get an overview of its contents. Then read one chapter at a time and try implementing its principles in your daily life. This is the time to work on the "Ask Yourself" and "How To Get Started" exercises at the end of each chapter. These exercises will help you pave your path to lasting happiness. As you work through them, the principles will gradually become part of you, and you will be able to live, breathe, and practice them intuitively.

1

DISCOVER YOURSELF

*To be born is to take a
seat in the school of life.*
                Anonymous

This section will address the following questions:

How can we discover all there is to know
about ourselves?

•

How do we begin to prepare
our mission statement?

•

How can we be alert and evaluate our
daily actions?

•

How can we constantly learn from our life
experiences and encounters with people?

•

How do choices create destiny?

•

How can we ensure that the choices we make
are consistent with our mission in life?

Define Your Mission

The indispensable first step to getting the things you want out of life is this: Decide what you want.

Ben Stein

I f we know who we really are, what we want in life, and how we want to lead our lives, we have a very good chance of accomplishing our aspirations. The articulation of who we are, what we want in life, and how we want to lead our lives can be called our personal mission statement.

Each of us has a unique mission in life. To discover our individual mission requires the willingness to embark on an inner journey – to define the personal visions and values that are meaningful to us. Writing a formal mission statement can bring clarity and focus to this journey. The mission statement reveals who we want to be and what contributions we want to make to society. It also clarifies the values and principles that must guide our actions if we are to achieve these aspirations. It encompasses the various roles we play as individuals and as family and community members.

Without engaging in this process of self-discovery, it is possible to go through a lifetime not knowing who we are and what our true potential is. The song "The Golden Eagle" by Anthony de Mello, in which the eagle dies believing he is a chicken, illustrates this.

In the song, a man found an eagle's egg and put it in the nest of a backyard hen. The eaglet hatched with the brood of chicks and grew up with them. All his life the eagle did what the backyard chickens did, thinking he was a backyard chicken. He scratched the earth for worms and insects. He thrashed his wings and flew only a few feet into the air.

Years passed and the eagle grew old. One day he saw a magnificent bird far above him in the cloudless sky, gliding in graceful majesty on the powerful wind currents with scarcely a beat of its strong, golden wings. The old eagle looked up in awe.

"Who's that?" he asked.

"That's the eagle, the king of the birds," said his neighbor. "He belongs to the sky. We chickens belong to the earth. It's not better or worse, just different, just who we naturally are. And the eagle is who he is, who he is born to be."

The poor barnyard eagle never reached his fullest potential, his majesty of the sky, because he had no idea who he really was. When we get to know ourselves intimately and unflinchingly, our sense of self-worth begins to grow. Each of us has great potential, but many of us do not use our natural endowments. Sometimes it is because our environment and upbringing, including the beliefs we have about ourselves that come from what other people tell us, put self-defeating obstacles in our path. We cannot help being influenced by outside forces. However, if we focus on looking in the mirror and seeing who we really are, beyond these influences, our self-confidence and inner power can grow. It is never too late. As long as we are alive, we have an opportunity to look in the mirror.

I began my journey of self-discovery by asking myself the following questions:

- What roles do I play in my life? *Parent, spouse, child, professional, employer, community member.*

- What do I expect of myself in each of these roles? *Empowering and inspiring parent, loving spouse, caring child, go the extra mile in my profession and business, be an asset to my community.*

- What principles guide me in achieving these aspirations? *Live with integrity, make a positive difference, live to my full potential, be respectful of others.*

- What is my burning passion in life? What activities challenge and stimulate me so much that I lose track of time when I am doing them? What kind of work makes me feel really worthwhile, in which I am making a difference and loving every moment? *Doing volunteer work, making a difference in people's life, giving motivational talks and writing inspirational work.*

- What are my unique strengths? *Positive, energetic, inspiring, and determined.*

- If I died today, how would I like to be remembered? What would I wish my obituary to say? *Loving, kind, generous, role model, made a difference.*

From grappling with these questions I arrived at my mission statement which is as follows:

My mission is to live with integrity and to make a positive difference in the lives of others; to live a balanced life and to enjoy the process of life. I seek to live to my fullest potential and to be at all times a role model worth emulating for my family, friends, associates, clients, and all who come in contact with me. I endeavor to always be thankful for what I have and to remember that whatever success I have had is through Divine grace.

Personal mission statements are not created overnight; be patient. The articulation of my statement took me several months of soul search-ing. The process of knowing oneself can take a long time – it is a far more complex process than it appears to be on the surface. Yet it is an impor-tant discovery in life, one that is essential in creating the happiness we desire.

Once established, the mission statement needs to be internalized. Ideally, we live it, feel it, and breathe it so that it becomes part of us. One way to encourage this is to read it twice a day – in the morning and evening – and to reflect on it. Although I strive diligently to live up to my mission statement, I still have a long way to go before I can live and breathe it. My mission statement is a star I aspire to, not a pebble I possess. What is most important is that I have clarity of my mission and am trying my best to live by it. If I am struggling with a decision, I look at my mission statement as my guide toward what really matters. My commitment to live up to my mission statement enriches and invigorates my life. This is an important process in the quest for true and lasting happiness.

ASK YOURSELF:

What roles do I play in my life?

What do I expect of myself in each of these roles?

What principles guide me in achieving these aspirations?

What is my burning passion in life? What activities challenge and stimulate me so much that I lose track of time when I am doing them? What kind of work makes me feel really worthwhile, in which I am making a difference and loving every moment?

What are my unique strengths?

If I died today, how would I like to be remembered? What would I wish my obituary to say?

HOW TO GET STARTED:

Pretend you will be given all the help you need to accomplish whatever aspirations you have in your life, but you need to write them down in a few lines. Write down how you would like your life to be. Consider how you would like to be remembered at your deathbed. This will give you a glimpse of the kind of life you want to lead.

Take a reflective journey and begin the process of writing your mission statement.

Keep revisiting and writing your mission statement after reading each chapter in this book. Aim to complete your mission statement by the time you finish the book. This is the hardest – but most worthwhile – exercise in the book.

Be Aware

Our mission statement clarifies and focuses our vision and aspirations. Once we have a clear idea of these, we need to start evaluating whether we are actually living in tune with our mission. Being aware means being conscious of our everyday motivations, actions, and responses. It allows us to discover the gap between how we want to lead our lives and how we actually do.

Keeping a daily journal teaches us about ourselves

A helpful way to gain insight into ourselves is to keep a daily journal. This is a useful tool for revealing what is really happening in our lives, as opposed to what we think is happening. It also allows us to better evaluate our motives, reactions, shortcomings, and strengths. Keeping a journal is like having a video camera around us that constantly records our behavior.

Writing in my daily journal has helped me immeasurably in the process of being aware. Through this practice, I have been able to capture the meaning of what is transpiring in my life much more clearly than before. I always thought that I was patient and understanding, but my observations gleaned through keeping a journal sometimes reveal the opposite. While writing about my daily experiences, I've noticed how impatient I can sometimes become with others, as well as insensitive to their feelings. It has been an eye-opener for me to observe myself doing the same things I implore others not to do. This understanding of myself has helped me be on guard, thus enabling me to gradually diminish and eradicate my weaknesses. Through this practice, I have also come to realize that I can more effectively work on a weakness when I am aware of the problem and can put my mind to work on it.

Being aware helps us recognize our shortcomings and capitalize on our strengths

The key to effectively keeping a journal is to make an objective evaluation of our behavior and commit to making the necessary improvements that will support our mission and purpose in life. Through the process of writing in a journal and reflecting on the choices we make daily, we can identify our weak areas or blind spots. Once we identify these weaknesses, we need to find out their root causes. One way of doing this is to observe when we indulge in this behavior and figure out there and then what triggered it. By being vigilant, we aid our understanding of ourselves and our ability to work on the problems.

Through keeping a daily journal, I have observed the following about myself, determined the causes of these behaviors, and am trying to find ways of improving these areas of my life:

- Occasionally, I have a difficult time controlling my temper. When this happens, I sense my lack of balance and composure. I've discovered that I tend to lose my temper when I am trying to tackle too much at once, and the pressure and stress of this causes me to lose my calm.

- At times, I find it difficult to relax. During these times, I rush through my day and don't take time to savor the beautiful moments of life. I have discovered that happiness is derived from the moment-to-moment process of living life. Every moment of every day presents a precious opportunity to be happy.

Knowing our vulnerable areas helps us stay aware, thereby reducing our chances of getting off track from our purpose in life. As we work on our weaknesses, we also discover our strengths. Last Christmas, my wife and I were planning a holiday to the United Kingdom. Two days before we were due to leave, my wife realized that her passport had expired. My normal reaction would have been impatience and anger. However, being alert and aware of my shortcoming, I instead chose not to react in anger and calmly discussed the options with her. We decided that we would go to the passport office early the next morning to see if they could renew the passport in one day. We knew it usually takes five working days, but we felt the worst that could happen is that they would not renew it on time and we would have to postpone our trip.

It so happened that Vancouver had a heavy snowfall that day, which made it difficult driving to the passport office. We somehow managed to get there and found that there was no lineup at the passport office. When my wife made her request, the supervisor told the clerk, "You had better hang on to her; you're not likely to get many more customers with the weather being so bad." The passport was issued promptly. Aided considerably by the snowstorm, my calm reaction to the passport problem paved the way to a solution, and we enjoyed a wonderful day in the snow. I discovered that not only can I control my anger, but I can be loving and supportive instead.

Being aware helps us learn from others

Our daily interaction with people can teach us a lot. Exposure to different experiences and viewpoints provides us with new perspectives on life, which in turn broaden our outlook. However, to take advantage of all that others can teach us, we need to be alert and keep an open mind. In this way, our understanding of our own and others' behavior is enhanced. Another family example, this time an experience with my daughter, demonstrates how this can work.

I was upset with my daughter, Sahar, because she had left her room untidy. The more upset I became, the worse it got; she was in tears but refused to cooperate. The outcome was that we were both left feeling angry, the room was still untidy, and, to top it all off, I had set a bad example for my son who was watching this display. When my wife came on the scene, she went straight to Sahar and hugged her. She told Sahar how helpful she had been cleaning the kitchen, finishing her homework, and looking after her brother the day before. Within minutes, Sahar had calmed down and cleaned her room, and was happily doing her school-work. My wife's ability to create a win-win situation by empathizing with Sahar's feelings and giving her positive recognition allowed our daughter to preserve her self-respect and get the job done. In this situation, I learned about my own behavior, as well as my wife's strengths and my daughter's needs.

How we view events in our lives determines how we react to them. If we are optimistic, then our reactions to life incidents will be generally positive. How we react to situations involving others is a reflection of our way of dealing with problems – and not a reflection of others' actions.

Staying aware brings us fully into the present moment

When we are aware, we are in tune with what is happening in the moment. In this way, every new moment – no matter what we are doing – yields new learning experiences. To experience life to its fullest, we must employ all our senses, including our emotive and intuitive ones. Emotive and intuitive senses are those where we read the hidden message, where we learn from the unspoken word and from the language of the heart and the soul.

As our awareness of our life's experiences grows, we learn to recognize more quickly when we go astray from our mission, and we can respond appropriately.

By being bold enough to admit to our weaknesses, we pave the way to overcoming them. But knowing and admitting to our weaknesses is only half the solution. The other half of the solution is to commit ourselves to taking corrective action. Initially, it may be hard to face our weaknesses, but, as we undertake this process honestly, we will discover new facts about ourselves and others. These new insights will open the door for the true meaning of life to emerge and will lead to lasting happiness and contentment.

ASK YOURSELF:

How do I react to events in my life, especially negative events such as a flat tire or a cranky child?

Do I carry optimistic or pessimistic thoughts with me?

What are my strengths? How can I capitalize on them?

What are my blind spots or weaknesses? What do they reveal about me?

How can I anticipate pitfalls and use my strengths to ensure that my reactions and thoughts are consistent with my mission?

HOW TO GET STARTED:

Keep a daily journal in which you express your innermost feelings. Write for five to ten minutes two or three times a day so as not to miss out on the many rich thoughts and moments that inspire you daily. It is okay to write just once a day for a longer period if that is your preference, although, from my experience, you are likely to notice more things when you write periodically. Read your journal often to become intimate with yourself.

Take an hour to consciously observe your thoughts. Write down your thoughts during that hour. What do they reveal to you?

Write down one lesson you learned today from your life. Reflect on this lesson throughout tomorrow. Do this daily for one week of every month and see how your life becomes an invaluable experience.

Discuss your observations with your spouse or a close friend and get his or her perspective about your behavior. This can give you new insight into your real self.

Recognize that Choices Create Destiny

Men at some time are masters of their fates: The fault, dear Brutus, is not in our stars but in ourselves, that we are underlings.

William Shakespeare

Every day of our lives we make choices, and each choice we make creates our destiny. Wise choices create a happy and meaningful life, while misguided choices lead to unhappiness and a sense of futility – unless we learn from them and do not keep repeating them. If we wish to be happy, we should strive to make choices that are consistent with our mission.

Choices aligned with our missions determine the quality of our lives

It is true that we are born into particular family structures and social environments that shape our experience and foster our beliefs and attitudes, but beyond this, our lives are not predetermined. We have the power and beauty of choice. In 1963, Harold, my former business partner, left a comfortable life in South Africa and moved to Canada with his wife and three young children. His reason for moving was to provide his children with better educational opportunities. He struggled through difficult times in the early years trying to find his place in a new country, but he persevered and stuck to his mission, a big part of which was to make the future he envisioned for his children possible. Today, all his children are flourishing.

We choose our actions, but not the consequences

It is important to realize that, although we are free to choose our actions, we are not free to choose their consequences. Wise choices create meaningful consequences, whereas choices exercised without care or responsibility create painful consequences.

Last year I was a speaker on social issues at a youth camp. A young girl shared the following experience with me. A few months before, she had an argument with her boyfriend, and they broke up. The boyfriend, hurt and angry, met with his friends, decided to get drunk, and then chose to drive home. His friends did not stop him from driving, and he was killed in a car accident. This incident tragically illustrates how a multitude of choices exercised without responsibility can lead to painful and devastating consequences.

Making choices is not always easy. Sometimes right and wrong are fuzzy, and we cannot immediately be sure we have made the right choice. Sometimes it is difficult to make choices from among the many seemingly important options that come our way. This is where the mission statement helps. If we have clarity of our mission, then we can go back to it to obtain direction. We cannot do everything we want; so we need to make choices according to how they support our mission in life.

Life is not predestined

Life is not predestined. We are all blessed with the freedom to choose, and our choices create our destiny. There is a Sufi story in which ten men want to enter a house, and only nine find their way in. The tenth man must not say, "This is what has been ordained for me." He must instead find out what his shortcoming was that prevented him from entering the house. Success is not just luck; it is a result of the choices we make and the effort we put into actualizing those choices. We have been given freedom to choose. As we use our fullest potential to work toward our destiny, we create that destiny for ourselves and for others around us.

Terry Fox, the famous Canadian who ran across his country to raise money for cancer research, made the choice to turn his tragic illness into an opportunity to help find a cure for his disease. After the shock of learning of his illness subsided, he found himself deeply affected by the suffering of other cancer patients, especially children. One day, as he was leaving the hospital, his teacher gave him a magazine article on Dick Traum, the one-legged runner who had just completed the New York marathon. The article inspired Terry to run across Canada to raise money for cancer research – despite having bone cancer and a right leg amputated above the knee.

When he first started training, he couldn't even run a kilometer a day. But through hard training and perseverance he was gradually able to run twenty kilometers a day. He began his marathon of hope on April 12, 1980, and ran forty-three kilometers daily for the next 143 days before he was forced to stop because his cancer had spread to his lungs. He died on June 28, 1981, one month shy of his twenty-third birthday. His heroic run has raised enormous financial resources and public attention for cancer research. Terry said, "You don't have to do what I did – wait until you lose a leg or get some awful disease – before you take the time to find out what kind of stuff you're really made of. You can start now. Anybody can."

Mother Teresa taught the wealthiest children in Calcutta, India, for over twenty years while living near the poorest neighborhood. One night, while walking home from work, she heard a woman crying for help. As the dying woman fell into her arms, Mother Teresa's life changed forever. She decided she would do her best to ensure that this never happens again to anyone within her reach, and made the choice of spending her life serving the less privileged. Her contribution to this cause was phenomenal.

Nelson Mandela and Mahatma Gandhi were both lawyers who left their professions and sacrificed many years of their lives to fighting for freedom for their people. Their choices and sacrifices changed the destiny of their nations. The key to their success was their conviction in their mission. Despite many obstacles, they followed through with their principles and goals.

Every choice we make shapes our destiny and influences the destiny of others. Happiness comes from making healthy choices in tune with our mission and taking responsibility in exercising our freedom to choose.

ASK YOURSELF:

What choices did I make in the last twenty-four hours?

Why did I make these choices?

What were the consequences of these choices?

Am I convinced that my choices create my destiny? Every time I make a choice, ask myself, "Will this choice lead me to my desired destiny?"

If I am straying from my destiny, is it because of the choices I am making?

How can I ensure that my choices are consistent with my mission?

HOW TO GET STARTED:

Begin with an ideal destiny you want to create for yourself. Think big – you will be amazed how much you are capable of. Review your draft mission statement to help you know what you really want out of life. Make sure that the ideal destiny you are conceiving is consistent with your mission.

Be on the path to achieving your desired destiny. Ask yourself what kinds of choices you need to make to lead you to your desired destiny. Write down one or two that you need to carry out daily or weekly. These may include finding time to exercise, reading half an hour daily, saying a daily prayer, spending quality time with loved ones, incorporating fun time with family, or giving extra effort to your most important goals.

DISCOVER YOURSELF

We have begun the process of defining how best we want to lead our lives as individuals, family and community members, and in our careers. This exercise has forced us to take an inward journey searching for what is most important to us.

In this section we have covered the following key points:

- Know who you are, what you want, and how you want to lead your life. Invest the time to prepare your mission statement.

- Keeping a daily journal helps us evaluate our actions and behavior. Through this process we are able to compare our actions and behavior with our mission and work on the gaps.

- Being alert helps us learn from life's experiences and encounters.

- Being aware of our weaknesses or blind spots and identifying our many strengths help us from faltering.

- We are always making choices. When we make wise choices that are consistent with our mission, we create a better destiny for ourselves.

- We are free to make choices, but not free to choose their consequences.

- Life is not predestined. We are creating our own destiny as we choose and work toward that destiny.

2

MAINTAIN POSITIVE ATTITUDES

Happiness is not a set of circumstances. It is a set of attitudes.

Anonymous

This section will address the following questions:

How can we use our fullest potential?

•

Why should we focus on what we have?

•

Why is worrying about what others think a
losing proposition?

•

Why should we give others the benefit of the doubt?

•

Why is it that whatever happens,
happens for the best?

•

Why is suffering not always bad?

•

Why do we need to strive for positive pride as
opposed to being egoistic?

Bet on Yourself

No bird soars too high if he soars with his own wings.

William Blake

e all have enormous potential to accomplish our aspirations. However, many of us do not use anywhere near our fullest capacity, simply because we do not believe in ourselves. Ask yourself, if I do not believe in myself, who will? If we are going to bet on anyone, let it be on ourselves. Only we have the ability to create what we want in our lives. The key is to know what we really want and to believe enough in our ability to single-mindedly go after it, as illustrated in Jessie B. Rittenhouse's poem.

> *I bargained with Life for a penny,*
> *And Life would pay no more,*
> *However, I begged at evening*
> *When I counted my scanty store;*
> *For Life is a just employer,*
> *He gives you what you ask,*
> *But once you have set the wages,*
> *Why, you must bear the task.*
> *I worked for a menial's hire,*
> *Only to learn, dismayed,*
> *That any wage I had asked of Life,*
> *Life would have willingly paid.*

Creating a vision supports our potential to emerge

One way we can encourage our potential to unfold is by developing our vision. Our vision is a clear picture of where we want to be at some point in the future. Creative visualization, the act of mentally conceiving something we want in life, can play a key role in crystallizing our vision. Setting aside some time daily to use our faculty of creative imagination has the potential to bring astonishing results.

In 1974, when I traveled to England from East Africa, my goal was to get my Chartered Association of Certified Accountants (ACCA) designation. My childhood education was weak – not because of lack of opportunity, but rather due to my lack of will or desire to study. When I was accepted into a program in England to do my ACCA, I felt my goal was within my grasp. I achieved this goal by 1979, and at one point passed seven exams in one sitting – a record for the college.

However, when I came to Canada in 1980, I battled for six weeks to find a job, despite my professional credentials. I was staying with a friend, sleeping on his couch, and desperately hunting for a job. My situation felt hopeless. At that time, I visualized owning my own home, being married to someone compatible and family oriented, having a couple of children, and starting my own professional practice.

I started focusing on my strengths and telling myself that I was professional, hard working, and determined – and thus an asset to any organization. Day in, day out, I visualized that I had accomplished my aspirations, although there were some days when I despaired of doing this. But I hung in through those moments and today I have realized these goals. I am convinced that even if I had had different goals, bigger or smaller, they would have been equally attained through the power of visualization. What we conceive in our minds, we achieve. As Henry Ford, the founder of Ford motors said, "If you think you can or you think you cannot, you are probably right."

If we fail to realize our dreams, it is either because we lack clarity as to what we want or we doubt our ability to really do it. Creating our vision, thinking big, and persevering through obstacles are key ingredients in betting on the potential we have to make our dreams come true.

Thinking big allows us to grow in stature

If we think small, we remain small. If we go to the ocean with one bucket, the ocean will give us one bucket of water. If we go to the ocean with ten buckets, the ocean will give us ten buckets of water. So don't bargain with life for a penny. If we ask for too little or for something we don't really want, then that is what we will get. Thinking big is about recognizing our innate beauty and power. It is about coming to know our divine greatness, and this knowing nurtures and supports our belief in ourselves.

In 1994, at his inauguration as president of South Africa, Nelson Mandela said, "Our deepest fear is not that we are inadequate. Our deepest fear is that we are powerful beyond measure. It is our light, not our darkness, that most frightens us. We ask ourselves, who am I to be brilliant, gorgeous, talented, and fabulous? Actually, who are you not to be? . . . As we are liberated from our own fear, our presence automatically liberates others." The power of thinking big is in all of us, regardless of our background or socio-economic status.

Persevering through obstacles brings success

Along our journey of life we will come upon obstacles in the pursuit of our goals, but we must persevere and continue believing in ourselves. Obstacles in our path are only detours, not roadblocks. True success lies not in never failing, but rather in rising after every fall; every failure has a seed of potential success in its womb. A person who has never failed is a person who has never succeeded. Thomas Edison dreamed of a lamp that could be operated by electricity. Despite many failures and setbacks, he made his dream a physical reality through perseverance, clarity of thought, focus, and belief in self. Don't be shackled by obstacles or failure – they are only stepping stones for success.

Michael Jordan had a slow start to his basketball career. As a child he preferred playing baseball to basketball. In fact, his brother

Larry was a better basketball player than he was. In his desire to be better than Larry and due to his belief in himself, he persevered and is now retiring from basketball as the world's greatest player. At some point, he had to bet on himself before the whole world would start betting on him.

We can make a difference

Sometimes we are overwhelmed by life's many problems and feel powerless as individuals to effect any positive change. Margaret Mead once said, "Never doubt that a small group of thoughtful, committed people can change the world. Indeed, it is the only thing that ever has."

A human being's self worth and happiness is at its highest when that individual is working to his or her fullest potential.

ASK YOURSELF:

Am I using my full potential?

Do I know what I really want in life?

Do I believe I can achieve these goals?

If I were granted whatever I wanted for the future, what would I ask for and why?

What is stopping me from aspiring to and getting what I want? Am I afraid to be successful? If so, why?

What steps can I take to give me the skills to succeed?

HOW TO GET STARTED:

Reserve a quiet time daily to exercise your creative imagination. Choose a time and place where there are no interruptions or distractions. Find a place that works for you (e.g., a den, bedroom, bathtub, sauna, or basement). Consider this a very important activity.

During this quiet time, use your creative imagination to visualize what you want in life. Let your imagination run free without setting any limits. You may wish to use this time to picture the goals from the mission statement you started working on in the first section of this book. Write down these goals.

Next, start believing your dream to be a reality now. Vividly imagine yourself completing your goals. Mentally picture yourself speaking and behaving in the new role you desire.

Finally, begin to assume that you have accomplished what you have visualized. Translate your imagination into reality by actually acting out the new role you envision. Notice how your thoughts and behavior gradually change.

Count Your Blessings

Gratitude is merely a secret hope of greater favors.

Francois Duc de la Rouchefoucauld

There is much we have and much we do not have. If we focus on what we have, we feel adequate, complete, and happy. If we focus on what we do not have, we feel inadequate, lacking, and unhappy. To count one's blessings does not mean ceasing to aspire to higher goals. What it does mean is feeling a sense of sufficiency that attracts positive energies for further success – and the creation of even more blessings.

Don't overlook your precious gifts

Although we often do not realize it, each one of us possesses priceless gifts. James was a pauper who watched the king being driven around and pampered by his servants. He resented the king for his wealth and felt a deep sense of injustice at the fact that he was so poor he could not afford to buy the necessities of life. When James shared these thoughts with his friend Marsha, he was shocked by her reply, "But don't you know the king is blind?" Long after this revelation, James was left pondering whether he would rather be a blind, wealthy king or a pauper who had been blessed with vision. The world is full of beautiful colors, sights, and sounds. If we can see, hear, taste, smell, and feel, we already have much to be grateful for.

Stop the habit of constant craving

Twentieth-century society encourages us to always desire more material goods and achievements. Most of us recognize the truth of the popular saying, "The more you get, the more you want." This wanting and getting and wanting more never ends, and there always seems to be something else we need to satisfy us. Yet, how often do we focus on being thankful for what we already have?

I visited Pakistan last year where it costs the equivalent of one U.S. dollar per month for children to go to some schools. Yet, even at what seems to be a very low cost, there are still many children who cannot afford to go to school. I met a family there that works fourteen hours a day in the blazing sun to earn the equivalent of that amount per day. But this is not sufficient to even cover the rent of their home, and there are ten in the family to feed. It isn't that these people are not as happy as those more economically fortunate, but, when we compare their circumstances to ours, we may conclude that we have a great deal to be thankful for.

Even in our deepest loss, we may find someone with a similar tragedy

Sometimes, when our worst nightmare comes real, we feel there could be nothing more painful in the world. My cousin Nuri and her husband, Diamond, lost their eighteen-year-old daughter, Nadia, in a tragic skydiving accident in Calgary last year. The pain endured by these loving parents is unimaginable, but their twenty-one-year-old son, Hussein, has been their pillar of support and strength. A few months ago, Nuri and Diamond met a couple who had lost both their children in a car accident just a month earlier. This meeting had an incredible impact on them. They could feel compassion for this couple because they had faced a similar tragedy.

Having little if satisfied is better than having much if dissatisfied

When we are content, we do not need too much to be happy. There is a Sufi story told by Sheikh Muzaffar about a dervish who is praying. A wealthy person passes by and, impressed by the dervish's piety, offers him a bag of gold.

The dervish asks him, "How much gold do you have?"

The wealthy man replies, "A lot."

To which the dervish asks, "Do you need any more gold?"

The wealthy man says, "Yes, I do. I work hard every day to get more gold."

The dervish hands over the bag of gold and says, "You need this gold more than I do. A wealthy man cannot take from a beggar."

Be grateful for the little favors you receive daily

Let us start each day by counting our blessings. No matter what our circumstances, we always have something to be grateful for, however small or insignificant it may seem. Our attitudes and practices are what count, and these will open the way to abundant blessings. When we focus on what we already have, we expand our gifts and cease to feel ourselves lacking in any way. Jalaluddin Rumi, the great Sufi mystic, once remarked, "When we see a big white cloth with a black dot, what do we see?" If we focus on the black dot – that is, the things we lack – it begins to look much bigger than it really is.

When we count our blessings, we feel good about ourselves. When we feel good about ourselves, we tend to treat others around us better. When we are good to others, we feel even better about ourselves. Thus, life-affirming positive energy encircles us, and we transform our lives with kindness and generosity.

While it may be part of our mission to constantly strive to achieve our goals and ambitions, being grateful for what we already have brings serenity and contentment.

ASK YOURSELF:

How would I feel if today I was given everything I wanted or desired?

How would I feel after six months of possessing these things? Would I have other wants and desires that need to be fulfilled? How would these wants and desires be essentially different from my current ones?

How can I get out of this constant circle of needing and wanting, and start the process of giving and contributing?

How would I feel if I focused on what I had rather than on what I lacked? Would there be an element of contentment and happiness in my life that goes beyond material pleasures?

HOW TO GET STARTED:

List all the things that are going right for you in your life. Write down as many as you can.

List three situations that you are currently most worried about. Now assess what is the worst that can happen in each of these instances. What can you do to minimize or eliminate the worry? Act promptly to do whatever you can to minimize or eliminate these worries. If there is nothing you can do, then that worry is beyond your control. Move on to attend to other things that are within your control.

Every night before you go to sleep, write down (or make a mental note of) three things – big or small – that happened today for which you are grateful. Try to come up with three different things the next day. Every day brings new and often unexpected blessings. If you believe in these blessings and stay open to recognizing and receiving these, they will come to you. Try doing this exercise daily, and within a month you will realize the wonderful things that are happening in your life!

Don't Worry About What Others Think

There is so much bad in the best of us, and so much good in the worst of us, that it does not leave room for any of us to talk about the rest of us.

Anonymous

e cannot control what others may choose to think of us. What we can control are our actions, reactions, and self-approval. Worrying about what others think takes us away from our own center and deters us from living in harmony with our life missions. By constantly trying to win others' approval, we expend energy that could be devoted to ourselves and to our close ones, and we consequently lose control of our own happiness. Refusing to worry about what others think of us does not mean that we do not respect others or have concern for their feelings. It means that we are content to be exactly who we are and not what we think others expect us to be. When we cease to worry about what others think of us, we take control of our happiness.

Look within to find your true value

The whole world may think us remarkable, but that does not necessarily make us so. We need to look deep within ourselves to find our true worth, to determine whether we are living in harmony with our best and noblest wishes for ourselves and for others. Similarly, just because someone else says we are no good does not make us so. Shakespeare wrote, "A rose by any other name smells as sweet." It is better to be true to oneself, even if this may lead to unpopularity, than to please others by pretending to be someone we are not. If we have discovered our inner self, are comfortable with who we are, and truly believe in what we stand for, then we should stand by our principles, no matter what.

Janet, one of my clients, is a self-motivated woman with strong principles and ethics. Many people think that because of her outspoken opinions, she has a chip on her shoulder. In fact, she is humble, yet confident, and she knows this. Other people's opinions about her can neither change this truth nor alter her positive self-regard, and she does not allow them to affect her. Instead, she focuses on her good qualities, and, sure enough, over time her actions speak louder than anyone's judgments possibly can.

Listen to everyone but make your own decisions

There is no harm in listening to others, but ultimately we need t trust our own abilities to make decisions. A useful aid to decision-mak is to examine how the decision adheres to our mission and vision i There is a funny Sufi story that illustrates this point.

A fox was seen running away in terror. Someone asked was troubling him. The fox answered, "They are taking camels for labor."

"Fool," he was told. "The fate of the camels has nothing to do with you. You do not even look like a camel."

"Silence!" said the fox. "For if an intriguer were to state that I was a camel, who would work for my release?"

When we are in trouble, blaming others will not bail us out. So it is better not to put undue emphasis on others' opinions.

Knowing your value frees your expression and potential

If we live preoccupied with what others think, we seriously inhibit our potential. I used to sit in many board meetings not saying a word for fear of someone forming a negative opinion of me. Later I realized that by doing so, my contribution to the team was minimal. I had so much to offer but was afraid to express myself. As my confidence grew, I began speaking up more, and my true personality unfolded. When we speak our minds without fear of judgment or censure, we are most effective. We begin to see that our views and thoughts are important and that we offer a unique perspective. The more we value our opinions, the more others will. Self-respect and freedom of expression are contagious.

You can be damned if you do and damned if you don't

There are times when, no matter what you do, people will find fault with you. As Sa'adi, the thirteenth-century classical writer, says, "No one throws a stone at a barren tree." The following Sufi story further illustrates this point.

A good man commissioned a builder to construct and prepare a house to be given to the needy. The builder started work but soon found himself surrounded by people who wanted to learn how to build houses. The builder hired the most competent people. However most people found fault with those the builder chose to help him. He continued to focus on the objective: to build houses for the needy in the most effective manner. Eventually, one of his critics, a person who was more fair-minded than the rest, suggested that perhaps if he could prove his intention by facts rather than opinions, then they could be convinced of his intentions. So the critics demanded to see the authorization from the charitable employer suggesting the hiring of the most competent builders. But when the authorization was presented to them, it was found that none of the critics could read.

Thus we learn not be too concerned about others' opinions and to stick to our mission.

ASK YOURSELF:

Do I worry about other people's opinions? Are their opinions more important than my own or those of my spouse, children, and parents? If so, why?

How much energy and effort do I expend trying to change others' opinions of me?

Do other people's opinions change who I really am?

Can I recall an incident when I worried about someone else's opinion of me? Did anything positive come out of this worry?

HOW TO GET STARTED:

Make a list of people whose opinions you worry about.

Evaluate how important these people are in your life.

Think about what it would be like if you did not worry about what these people think of you. How would you feel about yourself? How would you feel about them?

Give Others the
Benefit of the Doubt

*Whoever listens to the backbiter is an accomplice
of whoever backbites.*

Anonymous

Many of us attempt to know others before we even fully know ourselves. We judge, evaluate, and assess others without complete knowledge and understanding of where they are coming from. It is difficult enough to know our own motivations, but knowing those of others is next to impossible. As we reflect on how different we often really are inside compared to what we reveal on the surface, we need to ask ourselves how it is possible to judge another person whose inner feelings and thoughts we are unable to see.

Often, we get upset with other people without having full knowledge of the facts behind a particular action or behavior. When we are not sure and tempted to judge someone else harshly, let us try looking for his or her most positive side. By giving people the benefit of the doubt, we are showing maturity and understanding – and hoping that they will do the same for us. Our attitude toward others is a reflection of how we view ourselves. When we see beauty, we are ourselves beautiful.

Our judgment of others reflects our judgment of ourselves

We are often so quick to judge others that we do not realize that some of the weaknesses we find in others are the same weaknesses we possess ourselves – which is why we are so quick to spot them. We can only evaluate others through our own inner frame of reference.

Recently, I was putting my best effort into being a team player at home, and was consequently doing more work than usual in the house. I began to notice my wife, Farzana, taking it easy and not doing her share of the work, and formed a mental judgment of her that was quite unsettling. I carried that opinion of her within me for some time, and everything she did seemed to be wrong and further confirmed my judgment. The moment I let go of my opinion of her, I began to recognize the reality of things.

A few days later, we were having company at home and I watched in awe as Farzana took care of everything – from cleaning the house, cooking the meal, and setting the table to taking care of our children – while I continued with my work assignments. She did this naturally and without complaining. This incident reminded me of the years when I was heavily involved doing volunteer work, when I did hardly any work at home and Farzana shouldered most of the household responsibilities on top of taking care of our then newly born son. I learned a valuable lesson from this experience: never form a judgment without taking the time to put things in perspective.

Get all the facts before drawing conclusions

Often, there are a number of reasons that prompt certain inexplicable behaviors or attitudes in people. The least we can do is to find out the facts before we judge someone.

David suspected his wife, Jackie, of having an affair with her coworker Mark. The more he brooded about it, the more his anger escalated, until one night he confronted Jackie with his anger and suspicion. He was stunned when Jackie explained that Mark had been diagnosed with terminal cancer and was seeking emotional support from her as he had no one to confide in. Mark did not want anyone else to know about his illness, which was why Jackie had hesitated sharing the situation with her husband. Mark passed away a week after this encounter. Following this revelation, David started looking at things in a completely different light. Whenever he felt himself forming quick judgments about people without understanding the deeper reasons and motivations for the behavior, he corrected himself.

Focus on changing yourself instead of trying to change others

It is easy to make excuses and blame others when things do not go our way. When we take responsibility ourselves, we take charge of the problem and pave the way to a solution. Excuses mean opting out; responsibility means creating a potential solution.

When I was making slow progress writing my book, I started blaming interruptions from family, coworkers, guests, and kids for hindering my progress. This gave me refuge from the real reasons the book was taking so long to write and perpetuated the problem even further. One day I realized that I alone was responsible for completing my book, and that using others as an excuse for not completing it was a cop-out. With the support of my wife, I went on a retreat to get some uninterrupted time to complete my book.

Judging others obscures our focus on the important elements of our lives and on staying true to our mission. It is like the driver who looks at everything around him except the road ahead – until he hears a bang and swerves into the ditch.

Just as judging others is unfair and futile, so too are our efforts to change others. The more we change, the more people around us will appear to change. In reality, they may not be actually changing, but our perception of them will have altered. The more we focus on changing ourselves, the less we have a need to judge others.

Condemn the behavior, not the people

There are certain behaviors that are morally and ethically wrong and that we would never support. However, if we are operating from a mature, deeper understanding and perspective of humankind, we condemn the behavior but give the other person the benefit of the doubt (or the mercy of compassion in extreme violations). We learn the wisdom in the saying, "There, but for the grace of the Higher Being, go I." People generally do what they do because they do not know better. No one is perfect. As Henry Ward Beecher said, "Every man should have a fair-sized cemetery to bury the faults of his friends."

If we lead our lives focusing on the good in others and overlooking their shortcomings, we attract a similar response from them toward us. As we continue seeing the essential goodness in others and giving them the benefit of doubt, we begin to see the goodness in ourselves, and people begin to treat us with more kindness and respect. This in turn raises our self-esteem and creates an aura of happiness around us.

Recognize the many different perspectives in life

Everyone looks at things from his or her own perspective. One way of helping ourselves maintain a nonjudgmental attitude is to remember that there are many other perspectives in life that may be different from ours. The following Sufi story illustrates that.

A wise man was widely reputed to have become irrational in his presentation of facts and arguments. The authorities of his country decided to test him so that they could pronounce whether he was a danger to public order or not. On the day of the test the wise man paraded past the courtroom on a donkey, facing the donkey's rear. When the time came for him to speak for himself, he asked the judges, "When you saw me now, which way was I facing?"

The judges replied, "Facing the wrong way."

"You illustrate my point," the wise man answered. "For I was facing the right way from one point of view. It was the donkey who was facing the wrong way!"

ASK YOURSELF:

Can I recall any incidents where I judged someone harshly, only to find my evaluation was inaccurate?

Can I recall any incidents where someone else judged me harshly, and was way off in his or her evaluation?

How do I feel when people judge me without giving me the benefit of the doubt?

How do I feel when I give people the benefit of the doubt? What is the worst that can happen if I am too generous in giving such benefit of doubt? Conversely, how do I feel when I judge people harshly?

When things don't work out, whom do I blame? Why? When I blame others, what happens to the solution to the problem?

HOW TO GET STARTED:

Assign the best possible interpretation to every event by giving others the benefit of the doubt.

When someone has upset you, put yourself in the other person's shoes and look at the situation from his or her eyes.

Try focusing on these strategies for a week. See what you learn from recognizing the variety of perspectives in the world.

Do Your Best and Leave the Rest

Everything comes to him who hustles while he waits.

Thomas A. Edison

Happiness derives from the peace of mind in knowing that we have done our best. While it would be nice to win and be successful all the time, in reality we cannot. The baseball team that wins the championship still loses one-third of its games. Winning is not always possible, although trying our best is. An important aspect in creating the conditions for our happiness is to focus on giving our best in everything that matters to us.

Put winning and losing into true perspective

Real life is not a game of victory and defeat, but rather one of living life with honor, decency, and civility. The joy is not only in the winning, but also in the striving. If we have a "win or lose" philosophy, someone has to lose; but if instead we have a philosophy that encompasses both winning and losing, no one has to lose. In life there are no failures or misfortunes, only lessons to be learned.

Give yourself the "Did I do my best?" test

At the end of an exam, a sporting event, or a day's work, the question we should ask is, "Did I do my best?" If we can honestly answer "Yes," then it doesn't matter what the outcome of the activity is. If we have done our best, we can forget about the rest. I call this the "Did I do my best?" test.

When my daughter, Sahar, started a new school, she worked very hard in the first term. My wife and I wanted to give her the best possible start in life, and we put a lot of effort into helping her with her schoolwork. Even so, at the award ceremony, Sahar did not make it onto the honor roll. At first, we felt disappointed, but upon reflection, we were comforted by the fact that she had given her best. So instead of expressing disappointment to Sahar, we commended her on her effort. Our positive response and encouragement spurred her on to try even harder, and the very next term she made the honor roll. She now aims to make the honor roll with distinction. The most we can expect from our children or from anyone is that they give their best effort.

Recognize the value of struggle in day-to-day living

Life is not a bed of roses; indeed it can be a struggle. Whatever our situation, there always seems to be something to worry about in day-to-day living – whether it be finances, children, work, or relationships.

Beyond these daily demands, we may go through other unsettling and traumatic events. Some of us lose our jobs or may be affected by a major change in the workplace. Our children may be having difficulty in school, or we may be in a financial crunch. These conditions aggravate the day-to-day struggle. Yet, as we mature in our understanding of our purpose in life, we realize that struggle is an inevitable part of life. In fact, it keeps us on our toes and makes life exciting and invigorating. We realize that we get stronger and grow in stature because of our struggles and the experience of overcoming them. Character is like a muscle – the more we use it, the stronger it becomes. Our self-confidence grows when we commit to doing our best in each situation that confronts us and witness the resolution of our problems through our positive attitude and efforts.

Worthwhile pursuits take effort but are satisfying

Effort need not mean pain. Working toward worthwhile goals can be satisfying. Remember, though, that there are no shortcuts in life;

anything worthwhile takes time to mature, be it a meaningful relation-ship, a satisfying profession, a creative project, or excellent physical fitness. Without patience and persistence, we are unlikely to accomplish anything enduring. As the great essayist, Joseph Addison, said, "If you wish success in life, make perseverance your bosom friend, experience your wise counselor, caution your elder brother, and hope your guiding genius."

When we give our very best effort in everything that is important to us, our lives become enriching and happy – in defeat as well as in victory.

ASK YOURSELF:

Did I give my best shot to whatever assignment I undertook today? If not, why not?

How do I feel about the quality of effort I am giving to the things that are important to me and that support my mission?

What are my reactions to "losing"? What are my reactions to "winning"?

HOW TO GET STARTED:

Say "no" to those endeavors to which you will be unable to give your best. It may be difficult to say no in the beginning, but once you see the results in the most important areas of your life, saying no will become easier.

Evaluate whether you are giving your best effort to those endeavors you are saying "yes" to. Remember the mental picture you created of yourself in the section "Bet on Yourself"? Try wearing the hat of this person all the time, and keep asking yourself if you are doing the best you can to translate that mental picture into reality.

Trust that Everything
Happens for a Good Reason

Every exit is an entry somewhere.

Tom Stoppard

L ife has its highs and lows. If we associate happiness only with our highs, we will feel unhappiness in our lows. We need to derive happiness from both our highs and our lows. Our goal is to strive for excellence and to aim high for worthwhile goals. Once we have given our best shot, we need to relinquish all worries about the result. If there are things that are within our control to change, we can try to change them; but when there is nothing else we can do, then it is wise to convince ourselves that whatever happens, happens for a good reason.

Trust in the good in even seemingly bad situations

Lasting happiness has much to do with coming to understand that things truly happen for the best, however unfortunate or difficult it may be to accept. When we are able to integrate this powerful concept into our attitude toward life, we can more easily discard any thought that enters our mind that is to the contrary. Our focus then shifts to searching for the constructive side of the mishap, or simply to accepting that, although we may not understand why it happened right now, its deeper purpose and value will be revealed in time.

My friend, Roger, was terribly disappointed when he lost the opportunity to buy the fashion store of his dreams because another buyer came up with more cash. He was depressed for a few months until one morning, while reading the local papers, he discovered that the business he had desperately been trying to land had folded, and the new buyer was suing the vendor for providing misleading information during the sale.

Recently, I was invited to speak at a seminar alongside an extremely well-regarded speaker. It was a rare opportunity that comes along maybe once every ten years, but it meant going out of town for a day. I almost agreed on the spot to the engagement, but I had committed to consulting with my wife before accepting any out-of-town engagements. Farzana was not enthralled with the idea because I had been away the previous two weekends, leaving her alone to care for the children and business commitments – and I had an additional two trips scheduled in the coming weeks. However, she realized that I did not want to refuse this engagement, so she agreed that I go. I could see that I did not have her full support though, so I delayed responding to the invitation to the point of losing the engagement.

At first, I was extremely disappointed, but then I took the approach that it was for the best. I rationalized that my wife does not normally react that way; she has in the past supported many assignments, some of which have kept me away from home for as long as thirty days. I wondered if there was something about this particular assignment with which she was intuitively uncomfortable. After accepting it in this way, I never spent a minute worrying about the lost opportunity. My wife's support was, and is, far more important to me than any missed opportunity.

As it turned out, a month later I got a call for the same assignment but without the high-profile speaker. The impact of my speech this time was far greater that it would have been had I been overshadowed by the well-known speaker. Things happen for a reason. Once we have given our best effort, it makes sense to say, "Everything happens for the best."

Sometimes magic is hidden in ordinary misfortune

We cannot know the future, so when something bad happens, we often panic and lose all courage. At times like these, we need to keep faith and believe that there is always a purpose behind what is apparent. Forty-nine-year-old Gisele Faubert was understandably upset when she lost her job because of illness. However, losing her job turned out to be the best thing that happened to her. Had she been at work, she would not have bought the magic $20 million-dollar lottery ticket she did at the time she did. Gisele's philosophy, "If something bad happens, something good comes of it too."

If we learn to believe that things happen for a reason, that there is a greater design at work in all our life experiences beyond what appears on the surface, our lives will become much happier. When we are living in harmony with our mission, we attract situations that are beneficial to us, even if at first they do not appear to be so.

ASK YOURSELF:

What is the worst thing that has happened to me this week?

Can I identify any positive things that came out of this misfortune?

What is the worst misfortune I experienced last year?

What came out of it? Were there any blessings or valuable insights gained from that misfortune?

HOW TO GET STARTED:

Train yourself to believe that whatever happens, happens for the best. Believe that you are on your way to reaching your destiny and living in alignment with your mission and that whatever is happening is leading you to that, even though it may not appear to be so.

Evaluate what good comes out of any apparently bad situation. When things do not work out your way, perhaps there is a blessing in disguise. It could have been worse, or the events may be paving the way for something good to come.

Turn Suffering and Sorrow into Opportunity

Evening precedes morning, and night becomes dawn.

Haafiz

At some point in our lives, we will all face some sorrow and some suffering. Either we resort to debilitating self-pity, or we try to turn sorrow and suffering into opportunity. When we analyze sorrow and suffering, we can bring meaning to them, thus helping us to see them in a different light. This new outlook can lighten our burden. When suffering comes, there may be something better in store for us. When a caterpillar goes into a cocoon, it is the end of the world for the caterpillar; however, it is the beginning of life for a beautiful butterfly.

We are deeply strengthened by suffering

Suffering strengthens us. The more suffering we encounter, the stronger our capacity to endure grows. Humans are blessed with great capacity. Earlier I shared the examples of Nelson Mandela and Terry Fox, both of whom suffered greatly and not only endured their suffering, but transcended it to realize something meaningful and noble.

Before Charles Dickens turned to writing, he earned money pasting labels on blacking pots. The tragedy of his first love affected him so much and so touched his soul that he turned to writing and became one of our greatest literary figures. Beethoven became deaf and Milton blind, but both of them overcame their tragedies and sought opportunities to do great works.

The suffering in tragedy can be transformed into something beautiful

I met Azim Khamisa after his twenty-one-year-old son, Tariq, was murdered by another youth in January, 1995. While speaking with him about this tragedy, he shared his mission with me, one that had unfolded after his son's death and which was the bedrock of his being. His mission helped him turn this devastating life incident into an opportunity. He formed the Tariq Khamisa Foundation in 1995, which aims to combat youth violence and stop the nightmare of children killing children. The striking fact about this foundation is that Azim formed it in collaboration with the assailant's grandfather and guardian. He stated publicly that, in his heart, he saw victims at both ends of the gun and that America had been robbed of both children.

Sorrow can be a springboard to triumph

When people put us down, it brings us sorrow and hurt. Here too is an opportunity to turn pain into gain. By striving to overcome my humiliation in the following situation, I grew to excel at a sport that has since given me much pleasure. I had moved to a new place in my home-town of Dar-es-Salaam and was trying to make new friends, so I went to play soccer. I was so bad at the game that the other players would not let me play and asked me to sit out most of the game. I was deeply hurt, and my self-esteem was in my boots. I went home and cried and stayed depressed for two weeks. Then one day I decided that I would do all it takes to excel at the game. I promised myself that I would wake up an hour early each morning to practice soccer. Two years later, I was the captain of the team. An incident that initially caused much pain resulted in far greater pleasure.

Suffering brings us closer to our inner self

In the midst of intense pain we can turn to our inner strength. Consider the example of an oyster. When small grains of sand get into the shell of an oyster, they irritate the oyster, and it tries to get rid of them. But when it cannot do so, it uses those grains of sand to create a lovely pearl. If there are irritations in our lives today, we can follow the oysters way and make a pearl. It may take patience to make the pearl, but it will be a pearl created with love and faith.

We can rise above our hurt

Our hurt is only as deep as our reaction to it. We can transcend our hurt. In *Man's Search for Meaning*, Victor E. Frankl wrote, "We who have lived in concentration camps can remember the men who walked through the hills comforting others, giving away their last piece of bread. They may have been few in number, but they offer sufficient proof that everything can be taken from a man but one thing: the last of human freedom – to choose one's attitude in any given set of circumstances, to choose one's own way."

Suffering creates a faithful disposition

Some situations of profound suffering, such as a death, can lead to faith in the divine power for comfort and answers. Suffering not only forms character, it exposes it. My friend Muzaffar used to be a heavy drinker, much to the strong disapproval of his father. When his father passed away, Muzaffar was devastated. He stopped drinking and smoking as his way of showing his respect for his father.

When suffering or sorrow befall us, we need to focus on what we can learn from this mishap and how we can turn this tragedy into opportunity, rather than falling prey to self-pity and despondency.

ASK YOURSELF:

How can I turn a minus into a plus?

Do I recall an incident where I turned my sorrow into opportunity?

Can I recall any past sorrow where I had the potential of turning it into an opportunity for growth?

HOW TO GET STARTED:

Think of one mishap that happened today.

What was your response to it? Could your response have been different? Was there a potential within the mishap for a learning opportunity?

Train yourself to be conscious of your responses to mishaps as you go through your day. Being aware and observant will help you in this exercise. This consciousness and awareness will better prepare you to react positively to mishaps which are bound to happen now and again.

When tragedy or mishap strike, look deep within yourself for opportunities for growth.

Shun Egoism and
Strive for Positive Pride

When did I become less by dying?

Rumi

Positive pride comes from believing in ourselves and in our immense potential. With this strong belief in ourselves, we can work toward actualizing this potential for the betterment of society and toward fulfilling our purpose and mission in life. Positive pride helps to solidify our confidence, poise, spontaneity, and creativity. It is the zest and gumption to go out and give our best. It enables us to give our full self to life without inhibition or trepidation. For after all, life gives us back what we give it.

Egoism is conceit or negative pride – the mentality of showing off and acting superior to others. When we have no respect or tolerance for others, we become so self-centered that we cannot see life beyond ourselves. We are so engrossed in our own little sphere that nothing else matters. We achieve our "success" at the expense of others and often belittle and exploit them in the process. Negative pride is shallow and temporary and stems from insecurity. It relies on our worldly possessions to give us power, as opposed to getting power from within ourselves. When we suppress our egoism, the inner life is born. For the flower in us to develop, the bud has to die, and for the fruit to grow, the flower must wither.

Negative pride can sometimes creep unrealized into our lives

Pride has a way of creeping in without us knowing. As a wise person once said, "Pride is less visible than an ant's foot on a black stone in a dark night. And do not think that bringing it out from within is easy, for it is easier to extract a mountain from the earth with a needle."

While I was in university, I was excelling in my academic and sporting activities. Negative pride was subtly creeping into my attitudes without my realizing it. There was a woman in my class who did not seem to be doing well in her studies, did not have any friends, and seemed in need of some motivation. Convinced that I was good at motivating people, I made it my sole purpose to try to motivate and encourage her. After all, I told myself, I had motivated myself from being last in school to being first in university.

So one day I plucked up courage and asked her out for coffee. She refused my invitation! At first, I said to myself, "Ah well, if she doesn't need help, then tough luck for her." Later, as I pondered her response, it struck me that she had actually turned me down! My pride took a beating from a woman who, in my opinion, was severely lacking in everything I believed I possessed. This is when I realized that my ego had taken over and that my offer to help her had been condescending. I learned a valuable lesson: it is vital to be sensitive, discreet, and humble.

Negative pride or ego will produce a "fall" sooner or later

If we continue putting other people down, we will have our own turn to be put down. Nasruddin, the Sufi, tells the following story.

A proud grammarian once took a boat ride. On the way, the grammarian asked the simple boat driver if he knew grammar. The boat driver replied that he didn't know grammar as he hadn't gone to school. The grammarian replied that he had wasted half his life. A short while later, the water got rough, and the boat started sinking. The boat driver asked the grammarian if he knew how to swim, to which the grammarian replied that he didn't. The boat driver remarked that all his life would be wasted since he would now drown.

Humility is a sign of maturity and substance

We all have our strengths and weaknesses, and there is no need to put people down simply because we have skills that may be more highly valued in our society. Mahatma Gandhi said, "A man's greatness is in his smallness." Humility reflects a deep understanding of our limitations. It is the realization that we ourselves have been created and are not the creators. A tree that is full of fruit will bow down. A tree that is barren will stand upright in empty pride. The roots of a tree are its foundation but are hidden and have no need to show off.

When we do commendable work, there is a higher force behind us, guiding us and using us as vehicles. Therefore, we need to refrain from egoism. Isaac Newton said, "I don't care what the world thinks of me. As far as I am concerned, I am a small boy collecting pebbles on the shore, whereas the whole ocean remains unexplored." The more we know, the more we realize how little we know.

Celebrate the success of others as your own

I used to get jealous of other people's successes and was quite competitive. This burned up a lot of creative energy and held me back in life. One day it dawned on me that these feelings stemmed from insecurity. I realized that there is enough for everyone; one person's success does not mean failure for another. When we celebrate the success of others and wish them well, we can appreciate and enjoy the success in our own lives.

Positive pride attracts positive energy and happiness. Negative pride or conceit attracts negative energy and unhappiness.

ASK YOURSELF:

What would happen to my pride were calamity to befall me?

How do I feel when someone puts me down?

Since pride is so subtle, how do I know if I am possessing negative pride?

HOW TO GET STARTED:

Treat everyone, regardless of status, with the highest respect, and see how the respect is returned to you.

Accept that you may be egoistic – most of us are, to some extent. By accepting this, you have a better chance of catching yourself in that mode and can gradually eliminate this tendency. Recognizing and accepting a shortcoming is half the solution.

Try observing your thoughts and behavior and getting frank feedback from someone who will dare to tell you the truth.

Know that by letting go of egoism you will feel lighter and happier. It is worth the effort.

MAINTAIN POSITIVE ATTITUDES

Our happiness is a matter of positive attitudes and does not depend on external circumstances. When we are confident yet humble, give people the benefit of the doubt, and focus on doing our best, we take control of our happiness.

In this section we have covered the following key points:

- If we do not bet on ourselves, no one else will.

- The only limitations we have are those of our vision.

- When we focus on our blessings, they magnify.

- When we cease to worry about what others think, we take control of our happiness.

- It is hard enough to judge oneself, let alone judge others. Therefore, give others the benefit of the doubt.

- All that can be expected from us is our best effort. Once we do that, we can relinquish our worries about the rest.

- As we start to believe that whatever happens, happens for the best, we release the energy that is locked up in regretting.

- Our reactions to and understanding of sorrow can help soften our pain and even enable us to turn our sorrow into opportunity.

- Egoism is a state of shallowness and immaturity. Confidence and pride are positive when they are devoid of ego.

3

HONE
YOUR
LIFE SKILLS

*Life skills are the
chisel and hammer
for the sculptor of life.*

Farzana Jamal

This section will address the following questions:

How can we best use our limited time?

•

How can we maintain balance in our lives?

•

How can we learn to enjoy and take pride
in our work?

•

How can we display leadership qualities in the
different roles we play?

•

How can we make a positive difference in
the lives of others?

Stay Focused

Those who spend their time on small things usually become incapable of large ones.

Francois Duc de la Rouchefoucauld

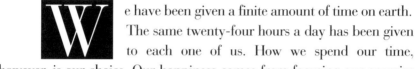 e have been given a finite amount of time on earth. The same twenty-four hours a day has been given to each one of us. How we spend our time, however, is our choice. Our happiness comes from focusing our energies on the things that we identify as important in life and that are aligned to our mission. If we try to do too much, our priorities become jumbled, which can lead to confusion, frustration, and unhappiness.

Focus on what really matters

The more we involve ourselves in activities that carry the greatest meaning and value for us, the greater are our chances for experiencing real growth. This may mean giving up some, perhaps many, of the things we are habitually involved in. By doing fewer of these nonessential activities, we free up more time for the essentials. We increasingly focus on areas that are consistent with our goals, objectives, and purpose in life.

Clarity of choice comes from our mission statement

Our mission allows us to distinguish between what is really important to us and what is not. It is certainly not always easy to focus on the important things; life imposes a multitude of demands upon us which makes focusing difficult. We have family commitments, professional demands, financial needs, volunteer involvements, and social commitments. Where do we begin? Whom do we say yes to? Whom do we refuse? It is easy to waver and neglect our priorities. But by doing so, by giving in to demands, pressures, and temptations that are not aligned with what we have identified as important to us, there is always a price to be paid. When you find yourself questioning the value of an activity, it is helpful to ask, "Is this what I really want to be doing?"

We can derive focus from an intense desire to reach our aspirations and goals. It is only by having a clear vision and passionate desire that we keep our focus on the essentials. When we single-mindedly strive to achieve our purpose, we have the greatest chance of success. This is because all our energies, drive, and concentration are centered on the task at hand, which frees our creativity and allows us to put a hundred percent effort into the task. Our mind, body, and soul are thus integrated in accomplishing our task.

Focus makes our tasks lighter

Ideas flow through our creative imagination when we have a clear goal in mind. For example, if the task is enormous, our focus allows us to break the task into pieces so that we are able to tackle a piece at a time. Our clarity of the end result and our concentration of energy help us realize that we cannot chew the whole apple in one bite.

By putting ninety-five percent of your energies toward the six or seven most important things in your life, you will see the difference you can make in these important areas of your life. The four areas in my life that I have chosen to focus on are family, health, spirituality (including service and writing), and professional and financial growth. And in each of these four areas, I have further concentrated on doing only what matters the most.

I used to get involved in all aspects of my business, from hiring and firing to maintaining records, client liaison, and administration. Our company decided to have a retreat where we brainstormed how we could take our business ahead by capitalizing on our strengths. This is where the idea was born that my main focus should be on management consulting for clients. The result of this is that my concentration, skill, hourly rate, job satisfaction, and profits have all gone up. Other employees also feel individually empowered as they have been given responsibilities that I previously tried to shoulder all by myself. Thus, less can mean more – much more.

When we focus on what is important to us and spend our time in areas where we can make the greatest contribution, our value to ourselves and others around us multiplies.

ASK YOURSELF:

What are the factors that guide me in determining how to allocate my time?

Am I able to say "no" to things I should not be getting involved in? If not, why not? What gets in my way?

If there were only three things in life that I was allowed to focus on, what would they be? Why?

HOW TO GET STARTED:

Establish your top priorities in life and ensure that time for these endeavors is not compromised at any cost. Look at your mission statement to identify these.

Schedule time for attending to these priorities before assuming any other commitments.

For one day, decide on the top two things you want to accomplish. Put the bulk of your effort into accomplishing these things.

The next time you are at a social gathering, try focusing on speaking with only two or three people rather than trying to speak with everyone. This does not necessarily mean choosing the two or three people whom you already know; they can be two or three people whom you have never met before. This way you can expand your horizon and outlook.

Live in Balance
and Harmony

Balance is the key to happiness.

Anonymous

e all have many roles and responsibilities, and when we are able to devote sufficient time to the ones we designate as most important to us, we can create balance and harmony in our lives. In the fullest sense, balance is achieved through the harmony of body, mind, and soul. It is the fusion of the different facets of life that renew each other and produce the synergy within us.

Balance extends beyond the material to the spiritual

The ever-pressing demands of our multifaceted roles and responsibilities in life – as spouses, children, parents, siblings, employees, friends, employers, and students – make it difficult to find everyday balance. In the hustle and bustle of daily experience, it is easy to lose perspective of what is most important to us and to get caught up in a temporal syndrome where we are so involved with our transient, material world that we have no time for the spiritual world. This lack of attention to the spirit affects our material life.

Attaining holistic balance requires us to look at life as a whole, not in its smaller, isolated parts. When we look at life in separate, fragmented compartments, we make decisions about and focus on things that are sometimes counterproductive to the well-being of our whole being.

Success in one part of life at the expense of another is questionable. If, for example, we have a drive to reach the heights of the corporate world but our focus in this endeavor is at the expense of spending quality time with our family and looking after our health, then we will pay a heavy price for that success.

Preparing a time budget helps us to balance

I lived an unbalanced lifestyle for about ten years. My time was largely spent in my professional and volunteer activities at the expense of time with my family and to some degree my health. I decided to prepare a budget of my time, identifying how much time I wished to spend on each of the key areas of my life, in order to find out what balance meant for me. This is how my weekly budget looked:

Family	28.0	Wife, children, and parents (17%)
Health	3.5	Walking half an hour daily (2%)
Prayer	9.0	Including half an hour of meditation daily (5%)
Service	7.0	Average an hour a day (4%)
Work	40.0	Professional consulting and writing (24%)
Read	7.0	Including newspapers and professional (4%)
Sleep	42.0	Average six hours a day (25%)
Plan	7.0	Average one hour a day (4%)
Flex time	24.5	Odds and ends and to allow for spontaneity (15%)
Total	168.0	hours

For one year, I summarized the actual time spent weekly in each area, evaluated its quality, analyzed the variance, and took corrective action. For example, initially I was spending time with my family just to meet my quota. But when I looked at the quality of this time, I realized that it was largely superficial. I was spending time with them for the sake of my schedule, and not always in ways that would nurture and energize these relationships. This changed when I began to ensure that family time was fun time. Now I invariably spend more than my budgeted time with my family because I enjoy and cherish that time.

One way I maintain balance in my life is to start my day early. The following morning schedule helps me to get ahead:

Wake up 4:00 a.m.

Meditate 4:30 a.m. to 5:30 a.m.

Walk and stretch 5:30 a.m. to 6:00 a.m.

Read 6:00 a.m. to 6:30 a.m.

Plan my day 6:30 a.m. to 7:00 a.m.

Waking up early and starting my day with meditation, exercise, and reading gives me a head start on the day. It ensures I have attended to my mental, physical, and spiritual needs by 7:00 a.m., giving me the whole day to take care of my social and economic responsibilities. I try to maintain this schedule three to four times a week. This schedule and this approach works for me, but it may not work for you. It is only one of many possible ways of living in balance and harmony. Each individual has to find out what works best for him or her.

Balance means different things to different people

Balance is different for each one of us. Since all our circumstances differ and we all have different objectives in life, our solutions to finding balance will vary. Balance is subjective. We may feel we are balanced, but those who are close to us and share our lives may disagree. Our responsibility extends beyond self, so at some point we may want to involve those who are close to us in the process of sharing time and prioritizing.

The key to achieving balance is to make sure we schedule our most important things in life into our day. I was talking to a single mother who had a hard time balancing her life. She managed to get better results when she committed to an hour a day for herself after the kids had left for school and before she began her workday. In that hour, she exercised and read inspirational books; the time was relaxing, energizing, and inspirational for her, and she managed to maintain this for five days a week. In addition, she scheduled half an hour a day for praying with her children and an hour a day for studying with them. The rest of the time was unscheduled and she went with the flow. By taking these small steps, she had taken care of the most essential things in her life and found a balance that worked for her.

These are only examples of ways to attain balance. There are as many different ways of finding balance as there are people. It is important to choose a way that works for us, and not to try force someone else's method or schedule on ourselves.

Our own innate sense of timing works best in maintaining balance

Beware of getting too caught up with the quantitative aspect of managing time and losing the essential value of the exercise. A watch is a useful thing, but it can become a hindrance. Relationships with loved ones are infinitely more important than the clock. Hanif, a friend of mine, shared with me the value of not wearing a watch. I thought it was absurd and unthinkable; I could not imagine operating without my watch. After all, my life revolves around time. I bill by the hour and schedule my appointments on an hourly basis. A few weeks after he suggested this idea, I misplaced my watch and was forced to operate without it for a week. The result was astounding. I reached my appointments ten minutes early, was relaxed, allowed my internal mechanism to guide me, and ended up getting more than usual done. Somehow I knew what I had to do and was no longer a slave to my watch. A week later, I found my watch. I now wear it but am no longer enslaved by it.

A truly balanced person is integrated, holistic, flexible, relaxed, and adaptable to change. As we attain balance in our lives, we become centered and feel complete. This state of harmony brings happiness in our lives.

ASK YOURSELF:

How can I juggle my many roles and responsibilities and still maintain balance?

What criteria do I use to evaluate whether or not I am balanced?

Do I allocate enough time for my family, health, reading, spiritual quest, and finances?

Do I manage time or does time manage me?

Do I attach more importance to my time or to my relationships?

HOW TO GET STARTED:

Identify your top priorities.

Allocate time for these top priorities.

When planning, expect things to come up that you did not anticipate. Some of these may be important. Therefore, allow some flexibility in the planning process to incorporate these opportunities.

Maintain a Healthy, Resourceful Lifestyle

Happiness lies, first of all, in health.

George William Curtis

Living a balanced life doesn't just mean balancing our time in terms of our relationships, work, and spirituality. It also means managing our bodies and resources. Our health and finances are integral parts of our personal resources and need to be managed well. Without good health, it is hard to enjoy happiness, and financial problems are one of the leading causes of stress and family breakdowns.

For a car to run well, the four wheels have to be aligned. Similarly, for a person to function smoothly, the four wheels – spirituality, physical fitness, mental aptitude, and social and economic well-being – have to be well aligned.

If one tire has a a flat tire or if one tire has too much air and the others have very little air, the car will not run smoothly. A human life operates in a similar fashion. Therefore, health and finance, along with spirituality, mental aptitude, and family unity, are important ingredients in the holistic approach to life.

Start with a simple fitness program

The human body is a complex mechanism that requires great care and nourishment. When our health is not up to par, it affects all the other areas of our lives. A simple fitness program is usually easier to sustain than a complicated one. One way to do this is to start with the invaluable free ingredients of fresh air and water, and top this off with regular, brisk walking.

After giving up league soccer and cricket, I tried many exercise programs, but nothing seemed to work. Last year, I started brisk walking, an activity that works especially well for me because it can be done virtually any time without much preparation or hassle. This takes care of my need for fresh air and exercise. In addition, I find that drinking six to eight glasses of water a day is refreshing and purifying. These simple steps make a major difference in maintaining my good health.

The key is to choose a health program that best works for you. Since we are all different, we will all have individual preferences. Our fitness programs can be as aggressive or as mild as we choose, provided we can sustain it and keep the other areas of our lives in balance at the same time.

Managing financial resources is a key to staying balanced

Lack of financial independence can get in the way of achieving and maintaining a sense of contentment and happiness. Good financial management lies in saving, self-discipline, and proper planning. I know some clients who make $30,000 a year and are debt free, while others who earn $150,000 a year are deep in debt. It is not how much we make that matters, it is how much we keep.

Jack has been a low-income earner for many years but is debt free and owns his home. He told me that his parents taught him one powerful lesson as a young boy: to save under any circumstance. He learned early on to save from his monthly allowance of $10 a month. This lesson has stayed with him all through his life and has been the key to his financial well-being.

Financial planning is essential for most of us to get ahead financially. It is said if we fail to plan, we are planning to fail. The basic process of financial planning involves setting short- and long-term financial goals; establishing net worth; preparing cash flow, budgets, and debt-reduction plans; and looking at insurance, retirement, and tax planning. Forming a habit of saving is also vital. Ideally, at least ten percent of our gross income should be put away by means of forced savings. The best way to do that is to have that amount automatically deducted and put into savings before we even see the money.

Good health and financial security are important ingredients to achieving balance and harmony in our lives.

ASK YOURSELF:

Do I exercise regularly?

Do I follow a healthy diet – one that includes plenty of fresh air and water?

Have I prepared a financial plan?

HOW TO GET STARTED:

Write down your short- and long-term health and financial goals. Decide how you are going to accomplish these goals.

Start with a fifteen-minute, brisk walk three to four times a week and drink three to four glasses of water daily. Gradually work your way up gradually to a thirty-minute walk and six to eight glasses of water per day. Alternatively, follow a similar weekly exercise and diet program of your own.

Decide on an amount that you can afford to save every month, and put that money into savings every month.

Work with Pride

Choose a job you love and you will never have to work a day in your life.

Confucius

Most of us spend a third of our lives at work. It stands to reason, therefore, that to be happy in life we need to be happy at work. Many people find this concept perplexing and, indeed, it is not an easy one to come to terms with. However, if we do what we love, in the final analysis we will always love what we do. Having a passion for excellence in our work brings about pride in our work. It is possible to make a living working at a job for which we do not have a real passion; but it is unlikely that this will bring us much satisfaction. If we seek success in a deeper, holistic sense, we need to work at something we believe in and have a true passion for. If we feel that our work is not important or making a difference, then it is difficult to acquire that passion.

Find value and passion in your career

It is not only what we do that matters, but also how and why we do it. Sandra is a hairdresser who lives in a small town with her husband and two children. She, like most women of her generation, spends a third of her day at work. She is proud of her family, enjoys good health, attends church, and lives a reasonably balanced life. A few years ago, Sandra believed that her work as a hairdresser was somehow less important than the work of her friends. Obsessed by these thoughts, she began to lose interest in hairdressing. After several years of dissatisfaction with her work, she finally went to see a counselor who discussed several options with her – including a career change.

In the next few weeks while she was reflecting upon her possible choices, new insights dawned on her. Sandra remembered how her sister had mentioned that her visits to the doctor friend were not pleasant and that he had on one occasion failed to recognize her son's ailment. Had it not been for a second medical opinion there could have been serious ramifications. Then Sandra recalled a conversation she had had with a client the previous week. Her client had shared with Sandra how upset she was with her lawyer friend because his fees had been excessive and his service and performance below par. Yet Sandra's own experiences with her doctor and lawyer were very positive and rewarding.

These occurrences reminded Sandra that not all professionals are good at what they do. Indeed, Sandra's counselor had emphasized to Sandra that it is not always what we do that matters, but also how and why we do it. The counselor had suggested that if Sandra decided not to change her career, then she needed to change her mindset about her work – and decide to excel at what she was doing. Sandra decided to work on this suggestion.

For the next few months, she identified the areas in her career where she needed to improve. She felt that she lacked good communication and listening skills and decided to take some training in these areas. She also attended seminars on building self-esteem and developing a positive attitude, gradually applying some of her new skills in her profession.

As Sandra began to take pride in her work, she noticed how she was able to make her clients feel better about themselves by the time they left her salon. Not only did she give them fabulous hairstyles, but she also made sure her attitude was pleasant and positive. The more she gave of herself at work, the more energy she created for herself. Sandra realized that it is easier to work with excellence than it is to work with mediocrity. By taking pride in her work she has made a difference to others as well as to herself. She has found that the happier she makes her clients feel, the happier she becomes.

As we become more self-aware, our interests and passions change

To take pride in our work, we need to do some soul searching to ensure we are in a profession or trade for which we have an intense passion. We must periodically evaluate how we feel about our work in order to ensure that our heart is in it.

When I was young, I was a good sportsman but not very interested in schoolwork. My parents wanted me to go into the sciences, but physics and chemistry were like Greek and Latin to me. I began to believe that I was not very intelligent, which affected my self-esteem and created a self-perpetuating vicious circle. A few years later I went to England and started studying for a degree in accounting, more by default than choice. I luckily realized that my interest was much greater in that subject than in the sciences, and I fared extremely well in accounting, both at university and later on in business.

After eighteen years in the accounting profession, I began to realize that I needed to do something different, something that would move my spirit and inner being. This is where the idea of writing this book was conceived. Now I enjoy both my accounting profession and my writing. All of us have varied interests, and these evolve as we journey through life.

By doing things a little bit better each time, we move toward achieving excellence. As Tom Peters and Nancy Austin say in their book *Passion for Excellence*, "Excellence is a game of inches or millimeters. No one act, per se, [is] clinching. But a thousand things; a thousand things, each one done a tiny bit better, do add up to a memorable responsiveness and distinction."

If we want to advance in any walk of life, we need to work with pride and attempt to excel in whatever we do. It is easier to work with pride than to work without it because, when we are able to do our best work, the work gets easier. As Edward Gibbon says, "The wind and the waves are always on the side of the ablest navigators."

ASK YOURSELF:

Do I view my work as just a means of making money? If I were financially independent, would I still be working in my job?

Do I have a passion for my work? Through my work, do I excel and make a positive difference in the lives of others?

What would it take for me to be the best I can be in my work?

HOW TO GET STARTED:

Any work that you undertake, personal or professional, should reflect a passion for excellence. Remind yourself of this daily, and internalize this habit by daily practice such that you will almost without thinking perform excellent work in anything you undertake. This needn't be only professional work, but can include work that is done as a volunteer and within the household.

Be a Leader

The mediocre teacher tells.
The good teacher explains.
The superior teacher demonstrates.
The great teacher inspires.

William Arthur Ward

Leadership is a valuable life skill because it allows us to move ahead in our chosen endeavors, especially those that involve working closely with others. We are all leaders in our own way, as parents, professionals, business people, community members, neighbors, or coworkers. Also, we may be leaders in some roles and followers in other roles. A good leader is also a good follower.

Leadership is about inspiring and trusting others

Drawing the best out of everyone, including yourself, is the essence of leadership. True leadership involves drawing from the inner strength of people, making everyone feel worthy, respected, and important. True leaders exhibit charisma, caring, kindness, and balance, and these traits draw people to them. Good leaders do not intimidate people; rather, they are approachable, centered, and happy individuals.

If we tell people what to do, they may forget; if we show them what to do, they may remember; but if we involve them, they will understand. Synergy, the merging of creative thought and energy, only happens when we keep an open mind and allow everyone's ideas to come to the table. Synergy results in the final outcome being far superior.

My parents are a good example of inspirational leadership. They led by example and never told my brothers and me what to do or what not to do. They had an unequivocal trust in us as children and an unshakable belief in our ability. All members of our family – no matter how young or old – contributed to making major family decisions. My parents inspired us by the way they led their lives and let their actions do the teaching. As far back as I can remember in my childhood, my parents spent an enormous amount of time serving our community in a volunteer capacity. People were always coming to our home for advice or counseling or help of some nature from my parents. My parents would always willingly give of themselves and considered giving to be a privilege rather than a burden. Parents play the role of chief executive officer in a family when they lead by example, inspire, and involve all members of the family in making decisions.

Good leaders are calm, thoughtful, and visionary

Effective leaders do not have a hustle-bustle, angry, or stressful approach. They are calm, thoughtful, and visionary. A calm leader inspires others to be calm and relaxed. When we are relaxed, we work with spontaneity, creativity, and optimal productivity. A thoughtful leader works smarter rather than harder. When a leader who is not intrusive, but knows how to delegate, empowers subordinates to be involved, gain self-esteem, and take initiative, it can only be good for both the individual and the enterprise. Otherwise, the leader ends up doing most of the work with very little input from others. A visionary leader naturally provides this vision to the team and develops it with the team's steady participation. An effective leader enlivens the vision by making sure that he or she clearly articulates the goals, objectives, and strategies of the team and that the team understands them.

True leaders give rather than take the credit

True leaders do not seek titles or recognition. Their greatest satisfaction comes when they see that everyone is happy and working to his or her full potential. They are quite happy to pass credit to the team and are generous in their praise of subordinates. An appropriate analogy describing a good leader is, "When it rains, the leader provides the umbrella; when it shines, the leader moves out of the way." When criticism is flowing toward the team, the leader takes full responsibility, but when praise and glory are forthcoming, the leader moves aside and lets his or her team take the credit. This is true and selfless leadership.

Leaders show foresight and are solution-oriented

Leaders are not fire fighters; they generally avoid conflict and reactiveness. They are planners and thinkers who anticipate problems and diffuse them before they happen – or else turn them into opportunities. Leaders turn minuses into pluses. Instead of focusing on where the blame should reside, they focus on what can be learned from a bad experience and how to prevent it from recurring. So, instead of wasting time going over and over the problem, they spend time finding a solution.

Leaders are naturally good coaches

When we are inspired, we can inspire others. When we are relaxed, we can create a relaxing environment. Leaders take this inside-out approach. They make sure that they "walk their talk," mean what they say, and have internalized the principles they hope to generate in the team. Leaders are natural coaches, and coaching skills and habits are part and parcel of their daily lives. Coaching aims to enhance the performance and learning abilities of others and involves providing effective feedback. Leadership is about catching people doing things right. Coaches motivate, question constructively, and consciously match each task to the readiness of the trainee to undertake that responsibility.

Leaders show understanding and empathy

Leaders are habitually excellent listeners who listen empathetically with their ears, eyes, and hearts. They are skilled at reading between the lines and listening, understanding, and responding to others. Leaders are able to constantly monitor the pulse of their team.

Leaders are superb motivators who inspire others to become great leaders. Leadership engenders leadership. I used to be a dominating leader at home, work, and other volunteer assignments. I thought I was being effective as I was getting results by running and controlling everything. However, my eyes were opened when I met Firoz Rasul, CEO of Ballard Power Systems and the President of the Ismaili Council for British Columbia from 1993 to 1996. I had the good fortune to work with Firoz for three years while I was a member of the Social Welfare Portfolio of the Ismaili Council. He taught me to lead by facilitating, engaging and involving others, empowering by consensus, and letting others run the show. I learned mostly by observing his leadership skills, and it constituted a powerful experience for me.

A true leader is thoughtful, examines the circumstances, understands the needs of the team, and adopts the best leadership style given a repertoire of alternatives. The same principles of leadership apply whether we are a business person, parent, coach, or CEO of a large corporation.

Given this understanding of what good leadership entails, in the next three chapters we will look at how we can become leaders. We become leaders by catching people doing things right, empowering others, and making a positive difference in the lives of others.

ASK YOURSELF:

Do I have a leadership role in some part of my life? If not, could I be a leader – as a parent, at work, in school, or at my place of worship?

As a leader, am I empowering or overpowering?

Am I a good listener? Do I listen to the unspoken word?

Do I find fault with others, or do I catch people doing things right?

Am I a good follower in roles where I am not a leader?

HOW TO GET STARTED:

Always look for the best in others, and show your recognition by a word or two to them. Drawing the best out of others is a great art that can be mastered with daily practice.

Begin by practicing leadership qualities at home – as a partner, child, or parent. Then extend this to other areas of your life – in work, community, and social endeavors.

Catch People Doing Things Right

When we see beauty, we are beauty.

Anonymous

When we catch people doing things right and commend them for it, we are noticing and affirming their strengths. This can help make them feel good about themselves. By encouraging others in this manner, we can also feel good about ourselves. We find happiness in seeing our recognition and praise help others and ourselves. Our society has a tendency to catch people doing things wrong, which can lead to increasing feelings of self-doubt and negativism.

Use praise to boost morale

When we praise people, it gives them a boost – an energy jump-start. This works with everyone, regardless of age. When my son, Tawfiq, is cranky, I find that, if I get upset with him, I perpetuate the problem; but, if I focus on his good qualities and positive behavior, he responds with more of that good behavior. By catching people doing things right, we encourage them to continue this desirable behavior.

Be specific and sincere in your praise

Everyone is positively affected by praise; but praise has to be sincere, not superficial, if it is to have the desired effect. Praise is most effective when it is specific; there is something commendable in everyone. No one likes to be criticized, so refrain from criticism for the sake of criticism. It not only does not help the recipient, but it is also counterproductive. If we must criticize, then it is important to begin with praise. It is less hurtful when we say the hard words in a gentle manner.

Once, while conducting a seminar on leadership to a professional group, I had the sense that my performance was rather mediocre and not having much impact on my audience. To my surprise, one of the organizers came up to me after the session and said, "You were really effective. You gave the right response every time you were asked a question, and you commanded respect from the group. Your command of language, choice of words, and conviction were great. The only area that you need to work on is that you should try to slow down and speak a little more softly." Her specific, constructive points meant a lot to me, especially coming after the sincere, positive comments.

Encouragement and love can change people's destinies

When we encourage and commend others with love, it is a of maturity and leadership and influences them for the better. In *Les Miserables*, the priest's support, love, and encouragement of destiny of the "outlaw." Because of the priest's love and kin outlaw gets a chance to reform and start a new life. He later becom best mayor the city ever had. He faces many misfortunes, but that one of kindness shown by the priest changed his life forever. The priest's love moved a social outcast to perform great deeds.

By catching people doing things right, we can create happiness in their lives as well as in the lives of those who come in contact with them. The more we praise others, the more praiseworthy we feel, for what we see in others is nothing but a reflection of ourselves. Seeing the best in others and recognizing them for their talents and abilities are marks of true leadership, well worth nurturing and developing in ourselves if we wish to fulfill our mission and attain happiness.

ASK YOURSELF:

Do I try to praise people at every opportunity?

When was the last time I commended someone?

Could I have praised someone today but did not?

How do I feel when someone praises me?

Have I been critical of someone lately? Could I have handled the situation differently with the same or better results?

How do I feel when someone is critical of me?

HOW TO GET STARTED:

Make giving sincere praise at every opportunity a part of you at all times.

Begin by praising yourself. Look in the mirror and tell yourself things you appreciate about yourself.

Do the same with your spouse and children.

Over time, extend this idea to your coworkers, employees, employers, customers, and friends.

Be liberal, yet sincere, in your praise and miserly in your criticism.

If you have to give constructive criticism, always begin by giving some positive feedback.

Empower, Don't Overpower

Give a man a fish and he will eat for a day, teach him how to fish and he will eat forever.

Anonymous

Essential ingredients of leadership are the willingness and ability to empower others. When we empower others, we respect and support their innate abilities. When we overpower others, we may be disliked and are ineffective. As we empower others, we are empowered in the process, which enhances our own satisfaction and happiness.

Encourage others to find their own solutions

We all know ourselves better than anyone else knows us, and we invariably know what solutions will best work for us. The best way to help people is to draw answers from them as opposed to offering advice. It is better to facilitate a response than to give an opinion or suggestion. Our role in empowering others, therefore, is to facilitate the process of helping them find the solution that will work best for them.

Last summer I wanted to prepare a timetable for my daughter because I disapproved of the amount of time she spent watching television. So I got onto my fatherly bandwagon, insisting she manage her time the way I thought was most efficient. Of course, all of this just went right over her head, and we were constantly arguing. Eventually, I decided to find out what she wanted to do in the summer and how she wanted to spend her time. As she spoke, I wrote down what she said. Then I asked her what she wanted to do first and how much time she wanted to spend in each activity. I then suggested she translate her plan into a timetable so that she would not miss out on doing any of the things she wanted to do. This approach worked like a gem. She ended up doing more things that summer than I would have ever thought possible.

Give people what they need to succeed and then let go

The keys to empowering at a group level are to involve the group in goal setting, take time to train if necessary, be available if required, and then let go. This method of leadership can produce astonishing results. I used to be the chairperson of a volunteer group. We invested time as a group to do some visioning and goal setting. Next, we ensured that we provided enough training to equip the members to accomplish the tasks they had set for themselves. We allowed the group flexibility to choose whatever strategies worked best for them, and then simply relinquished our attempt to control the results. The creativity, energy, and commitment this group displayed were far beyond our expectations.

To retain control, you must give up control

The more we let go of our control, the more in control we actually are. At work, I used to dominate all the decision-making; nothing would go out of the office without my scrutiny and approval. Employees were not allowed to make any decisions without first consulting with me. I was in charge and ran a tight and well-managed operation – or so I thought. I could not take holidays for any length of time, and, when I did go away, I would phone the office two or three times a day. The employees could not move without me. The emotional undercurrent in the office reflected low morale and a burned-out employer. I recognized that this approach was not working the way I wanted and took action.

Through taking courses on management and group dynamics and upon considerable reflection, I gradually realized that the best results come about when we empower others, not overpower them. This requires belief in the inherent abilities of people, a willingness to provide adequate training where necessary, and the skill to help others run the organization. As a result of this realization, I hired two managers to run my two companies, and every employee now has a say in the business. We have a profit-sharing arrangement, and our company has grown significantly. I have even been away from the office for as long as forty days without making one business phone call. This shift happened when I was able to give up my need to control the results and began to train and to involve the staff in the decision-making process.

As we encourage others to find their own solutions to the challenges in their lives, we respect their inherent self-worth. The more we do this, the more empowering we become. As we see the difference we make in their lives, our lives become easier, more relaxed, and harmonious, and we experience the inner satisfaction and joy that come from being a true leader.

ASK YOURSELF:

When I offer advice to someone, do I consider the other person's point of view?

How do I feel when someone tells me what I should or should not do?

How do I want someone to help me when I am experiencing a problem or difficulty?

HOW TO GET STARTED:

Whenever you seek to advise someone, begin by asking questions rather than giving advice and offering solutions.

Try giving people the available options, and let them make the decision by themselves.

Make a Positive Difference

I will walk this path only once, so whatever good I can do, let me do it, for I will not walk this path again.

Anonymous

A great quality of a good leader is his or her ability to make a positive difference in the lives of others – be it colleagues, employers, customers, associates, family, or friends. The good leader makes this difference through actions. Life is short, and if we keep postponing our good deeds, we may run out of opportunities to do good.

Belief and trust in the abilities of others create a positive influence

We make a positive difference in the lives of others when we believe in them, help them believe in themselves, and treat them honorably. My friend, Amin is a super soccer player. However, he had a very slow start to his playing career. His brother trained him, treated him with respect, believed in him, and helped him believe in himself. Eventually, Amin excelled at the game. His brother made a positive difference to him.

Our actions cause a positive or negative influence

Our actions speak louder than our words, and, by virtue of our actions, we can make a positive or negative difference in the lives of others. A few months ago, while walking in a quiet neighborhood, I reached an intersection at the same time as a car. I stopped, signaled to the driver to go ahead, and started walking behind the car. The driver snarled at me as if I had committed a serious crime. I was really upset by this because, after all, I was only trying to help the driver by allowing him to go ahead. Even though I should have ignored the incident completely, I was left thinking about it long after it happened. The actions and attitudes of other people affect us either positively or negatively.

Let us encourage and honor others. When we do this, we live our lives in a circle of positive energy, selflessness, and, ultimately, happiness. We can make a positive difference to our children, coworkers, neighbors, friends, and associates by showing them utmost respect and believing in their innate talents. Our greatest influence is not in showing others *our* richness, but rather in showing others *their* richness. If we succeed in making a positive difference in the lives of others, we feel valuable and instrumental in the lives of others, which contributes to our happiness.

Our positive influence lives beyond our death

My friend Shehin's sister, Yasmin, passed away at the tender age of nineteen. In her short life she left an indelible mark on people who met her. To this day her friends and family remember her pleasant and positive nature and her influence on them. Shehin is motivated to do good works through her sister's inspiration and her words of wisdom.

My aunt, Nurbanu, died of cancer at the age of fifty-eight. She was extremely ill for a whole year preceding her death. She knew the end was approaching, but, whenever we visited her, we were touched by her positive attitude. She refused to allow the sickness to dampen her spirits or the spirits of those around her. Her positive attitude endures beyond her death, she remains a great example to all of us.

ASK YOURSELF:

Did I make a positive difference to anyone today? How did that make me feel?

Was I negative to anyone today? How did that make me feel?

HOW TO GET STARTED:

Make a conscious effort to make a positive difference to those closest to you. Start by thinking of one or two actions that will bring a positive reaction from people close to you. As you implement this on a daily basis, it will become a habit. This will ensure that, by and large, you are making a positive difference to people dear to you.

Once you have started making a positive difference to those closest to you, extend this behavior to others with whom you come in contact. Eventually, making a positive difference in the lives of others becomes a part of your being. This helps you achieve your goal of being a positive role model.

HONE YOUR LIFE SKILLS

Life skills are the tools that help us live effectively. They enable us to attain success and happiness along the journey of life.

In this section we have covered the following key points:

- By focusing on our key priorities we can enhance the quality of our lives.

- Balance and harmony are achieved by doing less and scheduling time for the important things in life, including one's family, health, profession, spirituality, and finances.

- When we love what we do, we excel at our work.

- When we catch people doing the right things, they do more of the right things.

- As we empower others, we are empowered in the process.

- We are all leaders in some way. Leadership qualities enable us to climb the ladder of success.

- As we realize our true potential and help others work to their full potential, we find happiness and richness in our lives.

- Making a positive difference in the lives of others brings out the best in us.

4

BUILD
HEALTHY
RELATIONSHIPS

*We laugh and cry in
the same language.*
Anonymous

This section will address the following questions:

What are the key ingredients of a successful relationship?

•

What is love? Why is unconditional love so powerful?

•

Why can communication make or break a relationship?

•

How valuable are the people around us to our existence and learning?

•

Why is it okay to be different?

•

How can we maintain love and harmony in our families in our stressful and busy lives?

•

How can we value and nurture our children so that they grow up to be self-reliant individuals and assets to society?

Love
Unconditionally

I have spent my life, my heart, and my eyes this way: I used to think that love and beloved are different. I know now they are the same. I was seeing two in one.

Rumi

People define love in many ways – as a feeling, an energy, an expression, or a bond – depending on the context in which it is being viewed. In fact, the term "love" that is bandied about loosely and widely in our society ultimately falls short of what love means in a true or unconditional sense.

True love is unconditional

Unconditional love encompasses and transcends all other joys in life. The energy that flows from this kind of loving can indeed work miracles. Unconditional love is not based on performance or behavior but exists irrespective of all else. Loving someone unconditionally means deeply loving him or her without any expectation of what we will get in return. When we are able to love unconditionally, we overlook all shortcomings, forgive all trespasses, and wish others well. We love people for what they are and not for what we want them to be; we love them with all their imperfections. A mother's love for a newborn child is unconditional, as is our love for our pets. There is no thought of return or what the child or pet can do for us.

A Sufi story tells of a son killing his mother to get her life insurance proceeds. As he is hiding her dead body away, he falls down and hurts himself. To his surprise, he hears his dead mother utter, "Son, are you okay?" Despite his imperfections, the mother's love for her son lasts through death itself. She loves the child not because his actions are lovable, but because her love is unconditional.

When my then three-year-old son, Tawfiq, was in hospital suffering from asthma, I felt helpless but realized how deeply I love him. His illness made me reflect on the beautiful moments we had shared, the times I had put him to sleep while telling him stories, and how he had smiled with his eyes closed. I remembered the long time he took to wake up in the morning because he loved to hear me continue with my stories. I recalled the flashes of determination and joy on his face when we played soccer together. These memories made me realize that my love for him meant more than anything else in the world.

Unconditional love is intangible and selfless

Unconditional love is intangible. It is something we experience on a deep level but are not always able to articulate. As Rumi says, "The tale of love must be heard from love itself. For, like a mirror, it is both mute and expressive." When Princess Diana died, her unspoken love relationship with humanity unfolded, whereas before her death, the depth and magnitude of this love were not as evident to that amazing extent. As Antoine de Saint-Exupery in *The Little Prince* says, "What is essential to the heart is invisible to the eye."

There is no room for ego and control in the unconditional love zone. Like a candle that melts away, so will the ego melt away in the flame of unconditional love. When someone says, "I love you because you are mine," that is domination, not love, and the relationship is destined to collapse in the end. The total acceptance of the other in unconditional loving gently whispers, "I love you because you are you."

2
222

222222

Acts of love strengthen relationships

Building solid relationships means making time for those you love. Little and big acts done for our loved ones strengthen relationships manifold. My wife knew that I was having a hard time finishing my manuscript before leaving for an assignment in Pakistan. While I was away, for several nights she stayed up late after a full day's work and tending to our children's needs, and typed my manuscript for me. When she picked me up at the airport, she handed me my entire rough, hand-written manuscript now typed and ready for my approval. She has given me many other pleasant surprises in our marriage, which reinforces her unconditional love.

If we spend quality time with our children and love them uncon-ditionally, their beautiful potential will unfold like a flower and bring immeasurable happiness. Tiger Woods's father, Earl Woods, served in Vietnam and his assignments kept him away from his first wife and three children – eventually leading to divorce. Tiger was the only child of Earl's second marriage. Earl Woods had learned from his past experience and wanted to have a different relationship with this son. He spent quality time with Tiger, gave him unconditional love, and earned Tiger's trust and respect. By spending a lot of time with Tiger, Earl instilled the love of golf in him. Tiger knows he has gone so far in golf because of his parents. Earl Woods taught his son not only golf, but also the meaning and power of unconditional love.

Unconditional love arises from a deep spiritual understanding

Unconditional love arises from a deep and strong belief in the inherent goodness in every human being, as well as an understanding that none of us is perfect, that we are all one in love with no separation or boundary between us. With this awareness, we know that the truth of our being is love that is unlimited and endless. When we understand this, we simply need to remind ourselves that there is never any lack or scarcity of love. When we know that we always have enough love, we are free to love others abundantly and unconditionally.

Our experience of loving in a material sense – where we love with our incomplete and fragmented sense of ourselves, as a kind of "needs exchange" – is destined to bring us disappointment, disillusionment, hurt, and pain. It is only through understanding and embracing a deeper spiritual loving – where we recognize that we are whole, full, perfectly loveable, and adequate beings – that we can transform any limited experience of love and know abounding happiness.

Discipline does not negate unconditional love

Sometimes we need appropriate teaching to encourage children to improve their behavior; this does not, however, imply lack of unconditional love. William Shakespeare wrote, "You have to be cruel to be kind." If we have a child who is constantly misbehaving, we may have to teach the child to bring about appropriate behavior, and that is okay. Ultimately, the discipline will help the child negotiate his or her way into society. Discipline exercised with love is effective; it allows the child to see and feel the love and sooner or later to realize the purpose of the teaching.

ASK YOURSELF:

To whom do I feel closest? Do I love that person unconditionally?

Picture the person you love as he or she is right now. Now imagine this person is ninety years old. Ask yourself, "Would I still love that person?"

How will my present relationship fare in the face of calamities, traumas, and life-threatening health issues?

How will my love fare if I discover that a loved one has done something inappropriate?

HOW TO GET STARTED:

Try loving your children, spouse, and friends unconditionally by accepting them the way they are and not the way you want them to be. It is not always easy to do that. You may want to start by consciously overlooking some of their shortcomings and gradually accepting their whole being.

Sit quietly and imagine that there is enough love in the universe for everyone all the time, including yourself. As you begin to believe this, you will experience it within you and around you. The stronger your belief and conviction of boundless love, the more love you will experience. Feel this love overflowing and know that it exists equally for all, without any conditions or expectations.

Communicate Lovingly and Effectively

If words come out of the heart, they will enter the heart, but if they come from the tongue, they will not pass beyond the ears.

Al Suhrawardi

Communication can make or break a relationship. We have all seen many examples of broken relationships arising out of misunderstandings caused by lack of loving and effective communication. We have also witnessed strong relationships where deep bonds are forged through clear, honest, and trusting communication.

Effective communication is a prerequisite to happy and fulfilling relationships. This entails open, sincere, and respectful dialogue and keeping our minds clear of bias and presumptions. Effective communication is more than just words; our actions and body language often communicate far more than our words do.

Real listening is vital for good communication

The quality of our listening is an integral part of effective communication. Without active listening, communication is incomplete. When we listen actively, we listen with the sole purpose of understanding the other person; we listen with our heart, eyes, ears, and undivided attention. This requires a steady focus and genuine interest in what is being said and in the person who is speaking. Active listening is about giving the other person the space to speak and be heard – to simply receive his or her words before interpreting or evaluating them in some way. It requires a calm and patient attitude on the listener's part, a putting aside of our own busy thoughts to really hear what the other person is trying to say.

When we listen well, we understand. When we understand, we in turn speak effectively. Stephen Covey in his book *The 7 Habits of Highly Effective People* says, "Seek first to understand, then to be understood." When we first take time to listen and understand, there is a good chance that the other person, seeing our genuine interest, will also do the same when it is our turn to speak and will give us a chance to put our point across.

Communication needs to be regular to be effective

Effective communication requires a commitment of time on a regular basis. The most important gift we can give our loved ones is our time. If we do not schedule time for them, there will be no opportunity to nurture and develop the quality of our communication – and thus the quality of our relationships with the people most important to us. Often, our failure to communicate in close relationships is not through lack of desire, but through too many commitments that get in the way.

A family I know has committed to spending time with one another in an effort to improve their communication. Once a month, Chris and Sandra and their two children, Jason and Sarah, have an evaluation session where the entire family gets together in their recreation room. Using a flip chart and different-colored markers, they take turns to talk about the following:

- Three things that they like about each family member with specific reference to events that occurred in the previous month, and
- One thing that they dislike about each family member, again with specific reference to the past month's events.

They further suggest what they had expected from the family member in a particular instance. This exercise gives them valuable feedback that helps them to understand each other and gain new insights into what their close ones like and dislike about them.

Communication means sharing ourselves closely with other people

Along with scheduling time with our family and friends in order to foster and build the quality of our communication, we need to find ways of sharing our interests, motivations, desires, frustrations, goals, and dreams. Our neighbors, Lynn and Mike have scheduled a daily twenty-minute walk together during which time they have agreed to talk about the day's events, pour out their frustrations if necessary, and share a few laughs if possible. It is an all-round, win-win approach where they get their daily exercise, close time with each other, and a chance to unwind.

Close communication requires a willingness to be vulnerable

When we are open with others, we speak from the heart which makes us vulnerable because we may expose things about ourselves that are embarrassing or shameful to admit – even to our close ones. When we speak from the heart, we reveal our innermost thoughts and feelings, and when we are able to do this without fear of censure or rejection, we begin to experience true intimacy, love, and understanding in our closest relationships.

Peter found it very hard to share with his wife, Jackie, his attraction to slim women, but felt he needed to do so if he wanted Jackie to understand and accept him. After plucking up courage, he finally shared with her his attraction. At first, Jackie was hurt and angry as she took Peter's admission as a personal affront to her appearance. Peter felt vulnerable, exposed, and uncomfortable for a while, but, when Jackie decided to share her own weaknesses with Peter, their understanding of each other grew, and they achieved a higher level of intimacy.

Empathy is the key to communication

Effective communication involves empathizing with those around you. Empathy means going into another person's situation and living and feeling it in every way. Empathy brings about deeper understanding, and understanding leads to an appreciation of others. As we appreciate people around us, we create harmony and happiness in our lives.

Once, while I was meeting with a client, she broke down crying while talking about her child. Her child had been severely handicapped since birth, and my client had experienced much heartache rearing the child. When she shared her financial hardship and the sacrifices and insults she had to bear, I started crying myself. Then she told me how much she loves her child – and I felt every bit of that emotion. For the first time in my life, I felt and understood the meaning of empathy. Needless to say, my client felt and appreciated my genuine caring.

Communication can go beyond words

When we become really close, we have the potential of communicating intuitively. When we are really close, we understand a language that is beyond words. The following Sufi story illustrates this.

A merchant had a bird that he kept in a cage. One day, as the merchant was leaving for India, the land from which the bird came, he asked the bird whether he could bring anything back for it. The bird asked for its freedom, but the merchant refused the request. So the bird asked the merchant to visit a jungle in India and announce its captivity to the wild birds that were there. This the merchant did. However, no sooner had the merchant delivered the news to the wild birds in the jungle, than a wild bird just like his own, fell out of a tree and lay senseless on the ground. The merchant, thinking that this must be a relative of his own bird, felt sad that he had caused the bird's death.

When the merchant got home, the bird asked him whether he had brought good news from India. "No," said the merchant. "I fear that my news is bad. One of your relations collapsed and fell at my feet as soon as I mentioned your captivity." As soon as these words were spoken, the merchant's bird collapsed and fell to the bottom of the cage. "The news of its kin's death has killed it too," thought the merchant. Sorrowfully, he picked up the bird and put it on the windowsill. At once, the bird revived and flew to a nearby tree. "Now you know," the bird said, "that what you thought was disaster was in fact good news for me. The message from my relative, the suggestion how to behave in order to free myself, was transmitted to me through you, my captor." And the bird flew away, free at last.

ASK YOURSELF:

Do I have a daily scheduled time for communication with my family?

Do I make the time to communicate with friends?

Am I an active listener?

Do I listen with a view to understanding?

Am I appreciative of other points of view?

Do I openly communicate my feelings to my close ones?

HOW TO GET STARTED:

Attack issues, not people.

Say hard words in a soft manner.

Limit the number of spoken words to be effective.

Remain tender during difficult times. When you are angry or frustrated, take a walk round the block a few times, take a shower, listen to soothing music, read an inspirational book, or count to a hundred – whatever helps you retain your calmness.

Tell your loved ones often how important and valuable they are to you.

Value Diversity

There are many paths to the top of the mountain,
but the view is always the same.

Chinese proverb

e do not live on an island by ourselves but are surrounded by others. When we appreciate and value diversity, our intermingling with others becomes an enriching and fulfilling experience; when we don't, it becomes a miserable existence.

Each human being is unique. No two people in the universe are totally alike; even identical twins don't think and act in the same way. Since the beginning of time, there has never been one human being who is completely identical to another, nor will there ever be anyone in the future who will be completely identical to someone from the past.

Bridging our differences creates harmony and synergy

Our diversity comes from nature; it is what we are born with. It also comes from what we are taught and grow up with. Our different families, environments, educational backgrounds, cultures, traditions, friends, and social circles all influence the type of person we become. Within even one family there is much diversity. We are six people in my family – my wife, our two children, my parents, and myself. Each of us is so different from the other – different in personality, aspirations, attitudes, beliefs, and habits. The challenge is to find harmony within our differences so that the family functions smoothly and happily.

Each one of us has different needs and responsibilities, be they social, economic, physical, mental, or spiritual. Just as we try to integrate the various aspects and faculties within us to meet our personal requirements for development, so must we seek to bridge the differences in class, creed, boundaries, and religion of those around us in order to truly appreciate the diversity of humanity.

What a marvelous and complex world we live in! Difference is the beginning of synergy and is what makes synergy possible. Synergy is where the sum total is greater than its parts. We all have different talents and abilities that allow us to specialize in our particular fields and life endeavors and to share our contributions with others. For diversity to become a real strength, we must respect one another and understand that synergy arises from differences.

We constantly learn from each other through our differences

Diversity allows us to learn from each other because we use different strengths to accomplish common goals. Often we get irritated with people who operate differently from us. If we instead look at every person we meet in life as a teacher who can show us something we don't know, then each encounter can be a blessing – if we are only open to receiving the lesson. When we keep an open mind, become good listeners, and are respectful of others, we begin to treat each encounter as a learning experience, and life teaches us through others whatever we need to learn.

At my workplace, some people are organized and methodical, some are proficient in technology, others are tax experts, and others are creative and innovative. We all have something different to offer, and the ensemble of talents gives the firm diversified strengths and flexibility.

Diversity is about different perspectives and perceptions

When you look at a place of worship, what do you see? An architect probably sees the design of the building, a builder notices the strength of its structure, while a worshipper thinks of the sacred area itself. These are three different perspectives of the very same building – all of them correct and relevant.

These differing perspectives of life can cause much strife and commotion, sometimes culminating in animosity and war. Rather than looking at this beautiful diversity as a blessing and strength to humankind, we too often view it as a threat.

Aspire to experience unity in diversity

Most of us face somewhat similar challenges, hurdles, and obstacles in life. We may be on different paths, but common physical, emotional, economic, and spiritual needs and experiences bind us to the human family. Sometimes we confuse diversity with disunity, feeling that if we were united, we would not be diverse. The challenge for us, however, is to aspire to experience unity in diversity, and then what a world we would create!

Every living creature is a valuable soul. It does not matter if we are rich or poor, strong or weak, old or young, white, black, or purple; we are all created equal and deserve respect. What matters is that we are all human beings on a similar path of discovery. Seeking unity in diversity removes all prejudice, allowing us to look at everyone with fresh, nonjudgmental eyes.

Enjoy the variety and beauty in life's rich banquet

Differences make life more exciting and interesting; if everyone were the same, life would be dull and colorless. Imagine a garden with only one type and color of flower. We would quickly lose interest in such a garden. Alternatively, if there were flowers and plants of a whole multitude of colors and sizes, we could spend a great deal of time in such a garden, deriving joy, beauty, and inspiration in its variety. It would be ludicrous to be annoyed at certain flowers and plants for being different from others; we would accept and appreciate them all. Similarly, instead of getting irritated and perturbed by others, we can cherish and embrace different outlooks. How refreshing! There is a wonderful Native American saying that states that to really understand someone we need to "walk a mile in his or her moccasins."

The more we appreciate and understand others, the more we are appreciated and understood by others. When we love and respect diversity, life becomes profoundly enjoyable, rather than exasperating, experience. The more we take time to understand and value the differences in each other, the happier we become, as illustrated in the following story.

When Brother Bruno was at prayer one night, a bullfrog's croaking disturbed him. All his attempts to disregard the sound were unsuccessful, so he shouted from his window, "Quiet! I'm at my prayers." Now Brother Bruno was a saint, so his command was instantly obeyed. Every living creature held its voice, so as to create a silence that would be favorable to prayer. But now another sound intruded on Brother Bruno's worship, an inner voice that said, "Perhaps God is as pleased with the croaking of the frog as He is with the chanting of your psalms."

"What can please the ears of God in the croak of a frog?" was Brother Bruno's scornful rejoinder.

But the voice refused to give up, "Why do you think God invented the sound?"

Brother Bruno decided to find out why. He leaned out of his window and gave the order, "Sing!" The bullfrog's measured croaking filled the air to the accompaniment of all the frogs in the vicinity. And as Brother Bruno attended to the sound, their voices ceased to jar, for he discovered that, if he stopped resisting them, they actually enriched the silence of the night. With that discovery, Brother Bruno's heart became harmonious with the universe, and for the first time in his life, he understood what it means to pray.

ASK YOURSELF:

If everyone were the same, what kind of world would it be? What would be missing? How would that compare with what we have now?

What did I learn from others today? What could I have learned?

Did I judge someone harshly today merely because of his or her differences?

HOW TO GET STARTED:

Try for one day to put yourself in another person's shoes and look at life from his or her perspective. How does it change your reactions and attitudes?

Pay attention to the diverse characteristics and skills of the people you know.

Celebrate Family

The happiest moments of my life have been the few which I
have passed at home in the bosom of my family.

Thomas Jefferson

A family is created when anyone shares his or her life with another in a common environment. Although I have used examples of family that I am intimately familiar with, I do not exclude other types of familial relationships that exist in society. For the majority of people, although this certainly isn't true for everyone, the nearest and dearest people in our lives are generally our family members. When we treat them as such, spend nurturing time with them, and share our joys and fears with them, we find a true and enduring source of happiness.

Family is the heart of society which is made up of multitudes of families. Strong societies are comprised of strong families. Creating an enabling environment in the home and providing emotional support are the building blocks and keys to family unity and happiness.

Assign top priority to your most important relationships

A blissful marital relationship is a boon enjoyed by fewer and fewer people today. It is not easy to maintain a healthy and loving relationship in an environment characterized by a "pressure cooker" lifestyle, lack of tolerance and respect for diversity, and permissiveness. We need to be proactive and put the most important relationships in our lives first. This means setting aside time for communication, displaying unconditional love, and creating fun in our relationships.

By truly valuing diversity and accepting our family members for who they are, we cannot help but strengthen these relationships. During a recent trip to Europe, my wife discovered at the airport that she had misplaced one of our airline tickets to Lisbon. I was seething inside, thinking that if she were only more organized, this would not have happened. At the same time, I reminded myself that it cost only $90 for a one-way ticket and that surely my relationship with my wife was more important than the ticket. I reminded myself that she is normally very careful about keeping and organizing things and that I too have misplaced things in the past. Suddenly, something shifted inside, and I was no longer judging her. I calmly told her that I would go and buy another ticket while she searched through her bag again. Just before I bought the replacement ticket, she found the misplaced ticket. I was able to remain calm by accepting her instead of judging her, and I believe my calm disposition helped her find the ticket. My wife was touched by my reaction and understanding and told me so. This made me feel great, and I wanted to continue this attitude and behavior.

The practical challenges of our fast-paced lives will not disappear overnight, but by being alert and aware of our shortcomings we can transcend these problems. The reassuring touch, active listening, genuine caring, and open communication contribute to building healthy relationships.

When relationships work, they are springboards of energy, inspiration, and happiness that contribute greatly to our success. I was discussing this chapter with Stephanie, a passenger on a flight I took recently, and she shared with me something quite profound. She said that when your relationship with your partner is strong and well-grounded, everything else is a piece of cake. She also said that our time spent with our families and children is not a chore, but the very reason for our existence and a springboard for all success in life.

Judging from the current divorce rates, marriage is proving to be a major challenge for many. Marriage is certainly not the bed of roses the romantic myth purports. How can we reduce the chances of a marital break-up? One way is to understand the many challenges marriage entails before getting married. Marriage preparation seminars can help improve the chances of a successful marriage. These courses may cover topics such as communication, conflict resolution, lifestyle, financial planning, expectations and reality, and roles within the family. Marriage enrichment seminars after marriage can also help to enhance a marriage. I have been involved in organizing and facilitating such seminars in a volunteer capacity and know for a fact that they are effective.

Sometimes, however, despite our best efforts and intentions, our relationships break down. In such cases, an amicable and fair settlement is crucial, especially when there are children involved. Revenge and hatred between parents can cause lasting damage to children, and parents should do their best to avoid this for their children's sake at least.

Nurturing family roots creates enduring bonds

Our parents and grandparents provide our roots. Receiving their affection, love, and blessing is of supreme importance as we begin life, as is showing our appreciation and respect to them throughout our lives. We are an integral extension of our parents. Hence, we must do all we can to support our mutual well-being by taking care of our parents and grandparents. Our children, who are in turn extensions of ourselves, will then in all likelihood follow our example by nurturing and taking special care of us. Mutual respect, caring, and valuing constitute the glue that binds families together in strong and enduring ways.

My mother and father spent a lot of time and energy caring for my aging and sick grandmother. They fed, washed, and cared for her. It was a very difficult task because my grandmother was paralyzed and totally dependent on them. My siblings and I saw this devotion and caring on a daily basis, and it had a profound impact on us.

Shakespeare wrote, "How sharper than a serpent's tooth it is to have a thankless child." When we hurt our parents and grandparents, it is really painful for them, and we only realize this after they physically leave this world. There is a beautiful saying of the Holy Prophet of Islam, "Paradise lies at the feet of your mother." The abounding love of a parent is priceless.

Honor your close friends

Close friends can be an extension of the family, and we often share a bond with them that is akin to that of our own blood relations. The bonds of close friendship span time and geography. I had not met with or spoken to my friend Gulu for several years, but when I traveled to Houston for his birthday party, we instantly connected. I recalled my college days with him in Hampshire where I spent perhaps the most gripping five years of my life. Last year I exchanged New Year's wishes with my friend Rosie from Toronto with whom I had not spoken for nearly ten years, and memories of thirty years ago flashed back. The fact that I had not spoken to these friends in such a long time did not make a difference to the quality of the connection we share. It is most important that we cherish and honor our deep bonds of friendship, as they are lifelong and sustain us through good and bad times.

At the end of the day, for many of us, the people to whom we are closest are our family members – spouse, children, parents, siblings, and close friends. On our deathbed, we will always wish we had been kinder to these people, that we had loved them, and had spent quality time with them. We will not be sorry that we did not spend enough time at the office. Admiral Richard Byrd wrote on his deathbed, "At the end, only two things really matter to a man, regardless of who he is, and they are the affection and understanding of his family. Anything and everything else he creates are insubstantial. They are ships given over to the mercy of the winds and tides of prejudice, but the family is an everlasting anchorage, a quiet harbor where a man's ships can be left to swing to the moorings of pride and loyalty."

A healthy, happy, harmonious, and respectful family life is surely one of the essential ingredients of inner happiness.

ASK YOURSELF:

Am I comfortable with the amount of time I spend with my family and friends? If not, what am I doing to change the situation?

How do I treat my parents? Is it the same way I would want my children to treat me?

Am I expressing appreciation, understanding, and empathy to my partner?

Am I enjoying open communication in my relationship with my family members?

HOW TO GET STARTED:

Pick one of these suggestions at a time and gradually work through all of them:

Try to openly express your feelings. Do not bottle up feelings or deal with them in a secretive or hostile manner. Try first to calm down before expressing hostile feelings, but don't wait too long before expressing yourself.

Don't take your family for granted. Assumptions are dangerous.

Respect and value the differences in family members and friends. Everyone in the family has his or her own individual needs and rights.

Avoid getting angry at the same time as another member of your family; it takes two people to quarrel. Use the calming exercises suggested in the earlier section on communicating effectively. Remember, to be most effective, you should talk calmly when things have cooled down.

Deal with one issue at a time. It is hard to know what is really the issue at hand when speaking about several issues at the same time.

Pay one compliment daily to your spouse, children, and parents.

Let bygones be bygones. One way of doing this is to create a pleasant memory bank. Imagine the most favorable past that you can conceive. If you keep doing this, suddenly your past bad memories will fade away.

Plan your finances together. Prepare a sensible budget and share responsibilities.

Never go to bed angry with a member of your family.

Be aware of each other's goals and aspirations.

Slow down before you enter the house from a busy day. Relax before entering, so that you are in a calm mood. Try going for a walk after work, attending a fitness class, or doing some bird watching.

Nurture Children

*Your children are not your children. They are the sons
and daughters of Life's longing for itself. They come
through you but not from you, and though they are with
you yet they belong not to you.*

Kahlil Gibran

C hildren are the future of our society. They need to be
loved and nurtured to help them reach their fullest
potential. Having children is a tremendous responsi-
bility and requires energy and resources – but at the same time, they are
a source of immense joy and happiness and can give meaning to life. The
best gift we can give children is to provide them with roots – principles
and ethics by which they can make sound decisions in life – and wings –
self-esteem which will help them in all of life's endeavors.

We can supply our children with clothing, shelter, and food to
sustain their basic needs. We can provide them with the best education by
which they can claim their rightful place in society. We can try our best to
nurture them so that they are able to actualize their full potential. But
having done these things, we should ultimately let them be free to discover
and pursue whatever they choose.

Find ways to influence children without forcing them

Remember that there are no perfect parents. Parents fail not by
making errors, but by giving up trying to find a way to reach their children. I tried hard to get my daughter, Sahar, to subscribe to my philoso-
phies and beliefs, but she was getting bored listening to me and rebelled.
There was much silent frustration between us. Eventually, I changed my

approach and stopped pushing her. Instead, I played with her and tried to be her friend. At bedtime, I took the opportunity to narrate a blend of funny and philosophical stories to her. In this way, I succeeded in passing on my message to her in a gentle manner.

Tender loving care is the key ingredient

The gentler and calmer we are with our children, the more these qualities will resonate in their behavior. If we are respectful and considerate of them, they will be respectful and considerate of us. Recently, my wife and I returned from out of town after being away for two weeks. The day we arrived home, my daughter had a public performance and was quite tense about the responsibility. We calmly helped her with her preparation. During her performance I sat close to her to give her moral and emotional support. Afterward, I commended her courage and treated her to a dinner out. We really bonded at that dinner; she told me what she had done while we were away, and I shared with her the events of our trip. My gentle and caring approach helped her relax and release the pressure she had been feeling. It dawned on me just how much pressure our children go through. They receive far more homework than I ever did growing up. Homework, peer pressure, and all the other demands put on our kids cause stress in their lives. As parents, we can soften the impact of these demands by giving them tender loving care.

Trust, respect, and empower children to bring out their best

Each child is born with great potential. How the child is treated often determines his or her future. While genetic and biological inheritances influence who we are, it is by and large the amount of nurturing and love, as well as our environment and education, that determines the attitude and progress of the child. The manner in which the child is brought up will determine the type of adult he or she becomes. Children are to some extent like soft clay in a potter's hands. The beauty of the pot depends on the skill – love, care, and nurturing – of the potter.

Giving children broad guidelines for behavior with responsibility and accountability works far better than enforcing rigid rules. Our children need to be empowered, not overpowered. Generally, the more we trust them and show confidence in that trust, the more trustworthy they are likely to become. Keeping an open mind and listening with our eyes, ears, heart, and undivided attention is a powerful way to win their respect.

Being positive with our children and recognizing their good qualities at every opportunity can help them feel good about themselves. On Valentine's day, 1998, I wrote the following poems for my daughter, Sahar, and my son, Tawfiq.

Dear Sahar,
Happy Valentine's day!
Your energy, enthusiasm, and vigor are commendable,
Your deep love for the family blooms every single hour,
Spring is ever flowering when you are around.
How appropriate for Sahar – whose name embodies this message.
I get afraid when I see you grow so fast,
And gradually moving into your own world.
But grow as you may,
You will always be my baby, philosopher, princess,
"mumskin," bubbly, loving, caring, giving, laughing, darling,
and a million other good things.
After all, what is aging but maturing into deeper love?
I LOVE YOU,
Dad

Dear Tawfiq,
Happy Valentine's day!
You are an enormous soul in a small body,
You are the joy of my life,
You teach me the meaning of love,
You are my guru,
And I adore and respect you.
You are my sunshine,
Moonlight, and bright star.
I love you with all my heart's desire.
Waking you up in the morning
Is worth all the treasures of the world,
And hugging you is priceless.
My little prince, thank you
For being my BEST friend,
And I thank God with every breath
For giving me you, this invaluable gift.
I LOVE YOU,
Dad

ASK YOURSELF:

Am I providing "roots" and "wings" to my children?

Am I a good role model to my children?

Do I recognize my children's stress and give them tender loving care and the learning skills to deal with the stress?

HOW TO GET STARTED:

Put your children to bed with wonderful stories and take time to wake them up when they are young. As they grow older, give each child scheduled time for fun activities together and one-to-one sharing.

Allow a couple of hours a week to go out somewhere with each child and chat about anything the child wishes to share. See how this gradually grows into intimacy. Don't consciously strive for intimacy; let it come naturally, otherwise the child will sense an ulterior motive and not open up. During this time, be a good listener and keep an open mind.

BUILD HEALTHY RELATIONSHIPS

Relationships are the key to happiness. When we experience harmony in our families, nurture our children, and respect and value diversity, we find our lives to be happy and fulfilling.

In this section we have covered the following key points:

- Loving unconditionally transcends all that wealth and fame can bring.

- Communicating lovingly and effectively is the key to healthy relationships.

- Recognizing diversity as a strength.

- Celebrating the family and maintaining a harmonious and respectful relationship are important ingredients of happiness.

- Nurturing children can bring immense satisfaction and joy.

5

LET ETHICS
AND VALUES
BE YOUR
GUIDE

*There is no such thing as a
minor lapse of integrity.*
Tom Peters

This section will answer the following questions:

Why is it that the more we give,
the more we have?

•

Why do we get happiness from giving and
contributing?

•

Why does the "closed fist" end up with little?

•

How can a poor man be rich?

•

Why is happiness like a shadow?

•

Why are ethics and principles the foundation
of a meaningful existence?

•

Why do pure intentions breed action and
persistence?

•

In forgiving others, how are we doing
ourselves a favor?

Live Ethically

Character is the basis of happiness and
happiness the sanction of character.

George Santayana

O ur deepest joy comes from living an ethical life. Unethical living may bring temporary happiness, but it will be short-lived. Deep within each of us is a soul that is pure, which is why when we engage in pure activities, we experience happiness.

Ethics are more than simply a moral code distinguishing between right and wrong. For me, they carry a much broader meaning, which includes living a life guided by our principles, integrity, and harmony with our inner conscience. Ethics extend to living a life that is filled with love, respect, forgiveness, generosity, and kindness. Ethics also pertain to having a social conscience, being environmentally aware and friendly, and preserving the sanctity of life. Everyone deserves respect, irrespective of his or her status. Being ethical means having a heart big enough to forgive others for their shortcomings and truly understanding that "To err is human, to forgive, Divine." Ethics also extend to remaining nonjudgmental and refraining from gossip and backbiting.

Ultimately, ethics are not just prescriptions for living life; they have to do with obligations and responsibilities that are larger than ourselves and our ego and extend to our families, our communities, wider society, the whole planet, and all of life itself. As Emmanuel Kant said, "The greatest human quest is to know what one must do in order to become a human being."

Ethics are the baseline of our lives

Think of ethics as the backdrop against which we paint the picture of our lives. They are the foundation upon which we build the smallest and greatest of our accomplishments. Our ethics are like the number zero in our lives. We can only count numbers because there is a zero. Similarly, ethics are the foundation of our living; everything else we do emerges from them.

Dare to do the right thing

It is vital that our deeds, not merely our words, reflect our ethics. We need to crystallize our ethics in the practices of our daily life. Sometimes the distinction between right and wrong can become fuzzy, and in those cases, the intention behind the action is crucial. In life we are faced with two paths: the right one and the wrong one. If we take the wrong path, we may at first make great progress, but in the end we will face many disappointments. However, if we dare to take the right path, we may face many obstacles in the beginning, but in the end we will find happiness and fulfillment.

The time is always right to do the right thing. When we become entangled in doing wrong, the escape route gets narrower and narrower. As Shakespeare said, "Oh what a tangled web we weave when first we practice to deceive." We are sometimes unable to find a way out or muster up enough courage to change. Instead, we wait for what we hope will be the right time and the right moment and the right circumstances. But if we wait for the perfect opportunity, it may either be too late or it may never come.

My client, Peter, wanted to confess to his wife an inappropriate relationship he had with another woman while they were married. He knew that she would understandably be very upset, so he waited for the perfect moment to come – but it never did. As it happened, she found out about the relationship before he could muster up the courage to tell her. This nearly ruined their marriage. Since then, Peter does not hesitate or wait for the right moment to do the right thing.

Ethics are about keeping our promises and commitments

Being ethical means that if we make a promise or commitment, we must try our best to keep it. This story, taken from *The Tales of the Dervishes* by Idries Shah, illustrates this.

A man who was troubled in mind once swore that if his problems were solved, he would sell his house and give all the money gained from it to the poor. The time came when he realized he must redeem his oath. But now he was reluctant to give away so much money, so he thought of a way out. He put his house on sale for one silver piece. Included with the house, however, was a cat. The price asked for this cat was ten thousand pieces of silver. Someone bought the house and cat. The man gave the single piece of silver to the poor and pocketed the ten thousand pieces of silver for himself.

We all have our shortcomings. We should endeavor to identify areas where we are prone to falter and watch out for them in our every-day behavior. Awareness of our blind spots prepares us and reduces our chances of faltering. We can work on our shortcomings by exploring why we have them and what steps we can take to overcome them. If we remain ethical in situations where we are most prone to falter, we will find that we can remain ethical at all times.

Sooner or later, ethical choices work for the better

The end does not always justify the means. We may want to help our friends and do good, but we need to carry this out ethically. Sometimes the choices are not easy or straightforward, and we should endeavor to stay true and firm to our principles.

Alan, a friend of mine, once asked me to do him a favor. He wanted me to write him a reference letter of employment – even though he has never worked for me. This violated my ethical principles, and I told him so, even though I was not sure if he appreciated my dilemma. The choice I had was either to go ahead and help him, or to remain true to my principles and refuse his request. I figured if I was true to myself, Alan would appreciate me nonetheless, and perhaps even be influenced by my example. So I refused his request. Initially, Alan was disappointed but later appreciated my reasoning. We still maintain a healthy relationship.

Ethics encompass respect for the environment

It is important to be respectful of the environment at a personal, professional, and corporate level. Our decisions on all levels should reflect this respect and responsibility. There is an old Kenyan saying that, "The earth was not given to us by our parents, but has been lent to us by our children."

Complex ethical issues

Some ethical issues that touch upon questions of life and death can become extremely complex. These are controversial issues for which there are not always black-and-white answers. Ultimately, they are personal decisions and, at times, legal issues. What is important, however, is the process of decision-making around these issues, which must be based on good intentions and sound ethical principles.

Ethics and principles are the roots and foundation of our lives, the ground on which we stand. If we are to find the happiness we seek, we cannot afford to compromise on our ethics, and we need to be strong and steadfast in difficult circumstances. Living a life true to our deepest principles charts a steady course toward the unfolding of happiness in our lives, even if the path is difficult and full of obstacles.

ASK YOURSELF:

Do I have any frailties that lead to unethical behavior?

Am I engaged in any inappropriate activities? If so, why am I continuing to engage in these activities?

Am I waiting for the right time to change?

Can I decide to do the right thing now in some area of my life that needs attention?

HOW TO GET STARTED:

Start with honesty and integrity in the smallest of things. If you tell your child that you will take him or her to the park in the evening, make sure you follow through (or apologize sincerely and make it up). If you say that you will return a call at a particular time, ensure you do this. By learning to keep even small commitments, you will be better prepared when tested with larger, more difficult ones.

Have Pure Intentions

Happiness is a clear conscience.

Anonymous

very journey begins with a thought by which its course is shaped. The thoughts or intentions behind our actions determine what we will or will not achieve and actualize in our lives. If we believe strongly in what we want to achieve, then we will persist in action until we attain our goals. Intention without action is fruitless and shows a lack of commitment. Pure intention is the seed that gives rise to the action that results in worthwhile attainment. When our motives and intentions are pure and inspiring, we generate a great deal of energy that helps us overcome obstacles and challenges, and this enables fulfillment and happiness to unfold.

Our motives and intentions enhance our deeds

Why and how we do something are as important as what we do. Sometimes an action may appear worthy, but the intention is questionable. At other times, the action may not appear worthy, but the intention behind it is, as illustrated by the following example.

An artist showed his master what he thought was his best piece of art. The master said, "It is good, but it could be better." The artist worked twice as hard to produce an even better work. Upon reviewing it, the master said, "It is better than last time, but it still could be better." This happened several times, and the artist, after making repeated efforts to come up with a work that would please and satisfy his master, determined that the master must be jealous of his art. So the following week, he showed one of his paintings to the master, but told him that the painting was that of another artist. The master responded gleefully, "Why this is the best painting I have seen in a long time." The artist then revealed that the painting was his own work and accused the master of being jealous of his previous paintings. The master replied, "Now that you know you have done your best work, you cannot get any better. I was trying to help you reach your fullest potential."

Good intentions and actions can spring us to greatness. Terry Fox's intention to start his run for cancer was to raise awareness and resources to fight this disease. Terry passed away but his actions while he was alive live on in the form of others continuing his intention to accomplish those goals. His persistence in running despite his terminal illness and the steadfastness of his pure intentions are the cause of the astounding success of his goal. When our intentions are noble, we ennoble our actions. Noble actions create positive energy – which benefits us and everyone around us.

The energy available to us depends on our level of intention

If we work hard to become successful in satisfying our own needs, we are using one level of energy available to us. If instead, we work hard to become successful so that we can help our family and those who are less fortunate, then we have access to a much higher level of energy.

Intention breeds attention, and attention brings results. Just as we have to pay the price for anything worthwhile, we have to pay the price of knowing our real intentions. When I was in Pakistan in 1997, I had the privilege of working with Aziz Shariff, chairperson of Focus Humanitarian Assistance Pakistan whose mandate is, among other things, to repatriate and resettle displaced persons. Aziz invested fourteen to sixteen hours a day in this project with untiring zeal, enthusiasm, professionalism, and commitment. It was clear to me that his energy came from a deep desire to help the less fortunate.

Examining our intentions closely allows us to get in touch with our spirit

If you are unhappy with any situation or circumstance in your life, take a look at what your underlying motives are and see if you can align these more closely with your life mission. Some people manifest much energy even when their intentions are suspect; a thief will overcome many obstacles to rob a bank. However, it is difficult to sustain this energy and gain lasting happiness. Deep down within each of us is a pure soul, and unethical activity creates conflict with our underlying true nature.

ASK YOURSELF:

When I do not persist in my aspirations, do I examine my real motives behind those aspirations? Am I influenced by what other people think of me or do I stick by my inner motives?

Why am I engaged in a particular activity? Is it consistent with my mission? Does it lead to the realization of my vision?

HOW TO GET STARTED:

Always examine your reasons before beginning a task. Find out if it is a task that you have to do or if it is something that you want to do.

Always examine whether the task at hand will contribute to or take away from your deeper values and aspirations. If it will not contribute to your values, consider not doing it.

Forgive Wholeheartedly

In every pardon there is love.

Welsh proverb

At some point in our lives we have all been hurt by someone. Similarly, we have all hurt others, either intentionally or unintentionally. When we have been deeply hurt by someone, the scar remains for a long time. The deeper the hurt, the longer it stays and the longer the healing takes. One way to aid the process of recovery is to forgive wholeheartedly. Once we have forgiven someone wholeheartedly, we have begun the journey of recovery, of lessening the impact of the incident or hurt, and thereby retaining more energy for positive thoughts and actions. This paves our way to happy living. If we forgive wholeheartedly, we will benefit; if we don't, the grudge and anger will prolong our misery. When on the cross, Christ said, "Forgive them, Father; they know not what they are doing." We cannot all forgive as Christ did, but this is an example of wholehearted forgiveness in its most absolute and complete sense.

Forgiveness does not have to be direct

Sometimes we are not comfortable approaching a person directly to offer or show our forgiveness. At times, the person has moved away or even died. Here we have to realize that we can forgive in the confines of our heart or by writing down our contrition in our journal. When we do this, we feel a healing release, and the other person feels the energy of our forgiveness. Try this and see how you are able to release your negative energy and gradually feel the positive vibes from the person whom you are forgiving.

Emotional release is often necessary before we can forgive

Sometimes a hurt so deeply entrenched may require emotional release through counseling for the person to heal and begin to forgive. Here, professional therapy may be needed for someone to fully feel and release the pain of a trauma and be able to forgive.

Sandra's parents separated when she was nine. Each time her father visited the home, so great was the pain of his loss that she would cry for two hours in the bathroom after he left. Today, when the topic of separation comes up, the pain and hurt are still evident in her interaction, her voice, and her body language. She still finds it difficult to talk about her experiences and has not totally healed from the hurt caused by this separation. Sandra may need to revisit this trauma in therapy before she is free to forgive and move on with her life.

It is very difficult to forgive wholeheartedly – or even to forgive at all – in circumstances where we have been severely hurt either physically or emotionally. In these cases, we may need professional help and compassionate assistance before we can forgive.

Forgiveness allows us to move on with our lives

We are all prone to error. If others do not forgive us and we do not forgive them, then we would all be worse off. Seeking and granting forgiveness is a sign of humility and maturity. When I was young, I used to vividly remember every wrong done to me, and whenever I recalled the event or mistreatment, I would burn a lot of energy getting angry and hurt. After I read the book *How to Stop Worrying and Start Living* by Dale Carnegie, I changed my attitude by learning to forgive wholeheartedly anyone who wronged me in any manner.

As we learn to forgive wholeheartedly, we let go of the negative energy that blocks our spiritual development. The more forgiving we are of others, the more we free our energy to realize more of our potential for greater harmony and happiness.

ASK YOURSELF:

Is there someone in my life who has hurt me so badly that I have not forgiven him or her wholeheartedly? How do I feel about the incident?

Is there someone I may have hurt intentionally or unintentionally who may not have forgiven me wholeheartedly? How do I feel? Do I feel I should be forgiven?

How would I feel if wholehearted forgiveness took place in both these instances?

HOW TO GET STARTED:

When someone wrongs you, give the best possible interpretation to the event, giving the other person the benefit of the doubt. Say to yourself, "I am not perfect, therefore, I cannot expect others to be perfect." As far as possible, forgive wholeheartedly right away. When you have wronged others, seek forgiveness by apologizing sincerely and believing that they will forgive you.

Experience the Joy
of Giving

*You give but little when you give of your possessions. It is when
you give of yourself that you truly give.*

Kahlil Gibran

hen we are able to give and make a difference in
the lives of others, our lives become useful, worth-
while, and happy. When we are unable to give or
make a difference in the lives of others, our lives become shallow and
unhappy.

When we die, all that we have shall be left behind – be it our
wealth, health, knowledge, or worldly possessions. We cannot take any of
these to our graves. The Sufi mystics define a rich person as someone who
is able to give of his or her time, knowledge, wealth, and good wishes. So
someone who may be materially wealthy but unable to give, is very poor
in the eyes of the Sufi. *Mana ham jeb se fakir hai magar dil se ham Amir
hai* is an Urdu saying meaning, "Although my pockets are empty I am
indeed a very rich man in matters of the heart."

Unconditional giving creates abundance in our lives and spreads joy to others

The more freely we give, the more we will have. When we stop
giving, we stop receiving. If we have clenched fists, we cannot receive. The
moment we open our fists and give, we are also able to receive. This is
how the laws of the universe and nature work. In essence, the concepts of
rich and poor describe not how much or how little we have, but rather
how much or how little we give of ourselves.

There are many ways to give – we can give our time, thoughts, wealth, and guidance. Similarly, there are many levels of giving. Some give because they want recognition or medals or some form of return; it is better to give even with an ulterior motive than not to give at all. However, the highest form of giving is selfless and unconditional. Unconditional giving is when we give without any thought of reward, return, or recognition. It is far different from the bartering concept of giving – you scratch my back and I scratch yours – that exists in the material world today.

The best symbol of unconditional giving is that of a flower which gives its perfume, unasked, to every passerby. Even when you crush a flower, it still leaves its perfume behind.

There is a Sufi story about a poor, starving man who approached a saint and asked him, "What is my destiny?" The saint replied that he did not know the answer but that he would pray to find out. The next day, the saint told the poor man that there was only a bag of rice in his destiny. The man pleaded with the saint to request God to give him his bag of rice as soon as possible as he was starving to death. The saint prayed for his request. The next morning, when the poor man woke up, he found a bag of rice sitting outside his doorstep. Thanking his luck, he cooked the whole bag of rice and called his neighbor and friend to share the rice with him. By dusk, the rice was finished.

The next morning, the poor man found two bags of rice outside his doorstep. He continued his ritual by cooking all the rice and inviting more friends and neighbors, and together they ate the rice. By dusk, the rice was finished. The next morning, when he woke up, he found three bags of rice at his doorstep. When the saint asked God why the poor man was getting so many bags of rice instead of the one He had predicted, God told him that, because of the poor man's generosity in his poverty, he had changed and recreated his destiny.

Giving is a powerful way of creating abundance in our lives, but only when we give freely and unconditionally. We also invariably get back what we give. In 1992, I was appointed chairperson of a not-for-profit organization called Focus. The mandate of Focus at that time was to help educate children in the third world. It cost fifteen dollars to send one child to school for a month. My responsibility was to mobilize funds for this cause. I decided to begin this task with myself. I had a habit of buying a cup of coffee in the morning from the neighborhood corner store. I calculated out that if I did not buy the coffee, I would save twenty dollars a month. If I factored in the tax savings that I would receive on the donations, I would be in a position to send two children to school just by giving up a cup of coffee a day! I decided to quit buying the coffee, even though I could have well afforded the coffee as well as the donations. A couple of days later, I was driving by the store and caught a sign that read, "Free coffee with purchase of 25 liters of gas." In those days I used to drive a lot, so I practically recovered the coffee formerly bought.

It is not the quantity of giving but the intention and the thought that counts

When I was in Pakistan working with Afghan refugees, I noticed that despite their plight, they would always receive a guest in their home with the best food or offering they had available. It was quite remarkable to see their giving natures. It taught me that we don't need wealth to give, we only need a heart. When our hearts are open to giving, abundance in one form or another must surely follow. It is not how much we give that matters, it is the thought. Just because we cannot help the whole world, it doesn't mean we shouldn't still try to help whomever we can.

In *Chicken Soup for the Soul* by Jack Caufield and Mark V. Hansen there is a story of a local native throwing starfish in the ocean to save them from death on the shore after the tide had left them stranded there. When asked how he planned to save thousands of starfish from dying on the shore, he replied, while throwing one more starfish into the ocean, "Made a difference to that one."

Every minute is an opportunity to give, so let us make sure our positive influence is influencing whoever crosses our path for the better –

be it through a smile, a compliment, or a lending hand. There are many, many ways of giving, none less important or valuable than another. It is our willingness, openness, and attitude in giving that truly matter. The more of ourselves we share, the more of ourselves we find. When we help others, we open up space for help to come to us. Happiness is like a shadow; the more we follow it, the more it will elude us. If instead we work toward giving happiness to others, happiness, like the shadow, will follow us.

The beautiful prayer of St. Francis supports the joy of giving: *Lord, make me an instrument of Thy peace. Where there is hatred, let me sow love; where there is injury, pardon; where there is doubt, faith; where there is despair, hope; where there is darkness, light; where there is sadness, joy. O Divine Master, grant I may not so much seek to be consoled as to console, to be understood as to understand, to be loved as to love. For it is in giving that we receive; it is in pardoning that we are pardoned; it is in dying to self that we are born.*

ASK YOURSELF:

Do I give unconditionally of myself to close ones and others?

Do I feel happy for the success of others?

Do I wish others well?

Do I have an "abundant" philosophy? That is, do I believe that the more I give, the more I have?

Do I believe that there is enough for everyone and that someone else's gain does not mean less for me?

In what ways have I given of myself today?

Under what circumstances do I hold myself back from giving?

HOW TO GET STARTED:

Start treating every person you meet, regardless of status, and in whatever circumstance, with the highest respect.

Take every opportunity you can to make a difference, to give of yourself for the betterment of others. It does not matter how small the difference is.

Try to put yourself in others' shoes and think of what would make them happy. Try to get away from thinking only about your happiness, and focus on others' happiness. Then see how happiness follows you.

LET ETHICS AND VALUES
BE YOUR GUIDE

When we practice true giving and live an ethical life, we find inner happiness that is ever-flowing and eternal.

In this section we have covered the following key points:

- The more we give, the more we have.

- Happiness is like a shadow: if we try to follow it, it will elude us. If instead, we give it to others, it will follow us.

- If we cannot make a difference to everyone, we can make a difference to someone.

- Every day is a giving opportunity.

- Ethical living is the way to marry our material life to our spiritual life.

- Our pure intentions are the roots that give rise to persistence, success, and happiness.

- When we forgive wholeheartedly, we banish negativity and unleash our creative energies.

6

AWAKEN
YOUR
SPIRITUALITY

*The owl whose night-bound
eyes are blind unto the day
cannot unveil the mystery
of light.*

Kahlil Gibran

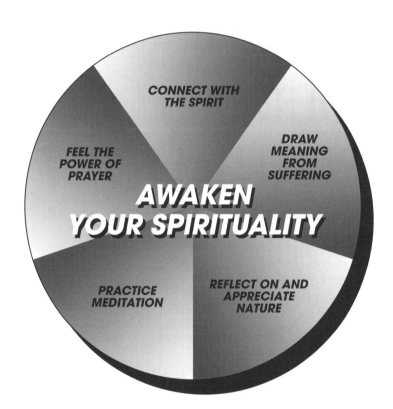

CONNECT WITH
THE SPIRIT

DRAW
MEANING
FROM
SUFFERING

FEEL THE
POWER OF
PRAYER

AWAKEN
YOUR SPIRITUALITY

PRACTICE
MEDITATION

REFLECT ON AND
APPRECIATE
NATURE

This section will address the following questions:

What is a spirit?

•

How do I connect with my spirit?

•

Why is a spiritual journey as important, if not
more important, than the material life?

•

What are the ingredients of spiritual
awakening?

•

Why is nature so powerful in giving us
spiritual messages?

•

How do we translate our material activities
into spiritual ones?

•

How can we experience the power of prayer?

•

Why is it so valuable to practice meditation?

•

What are the deep meanings of suffering?

Connect with the Spirit

Give up your drop and become part of the ocean.

Rumi

When we die, our body perishes, but our spirit lives on. Every living creature has a soul that is a part of the Divine Spirit that connects us all. The soul is vested within us, just like fragrance is vested in a flower. The soul does not die with our physical death, but continues on the spiritual journey. Unlike physical or material happiness, which is temporary and fleeting, deep and lasting happiness comes when we connect with our soul and develop our spirituality.

Sometimes we question the existence of the spirit. This is like a fish questioning the existence of life above water. In other words, although the spirit cannot be seen, it does exist. Not everything can be seen through our eyes, smelled with our nose, heard with our ears, or felt with our skin.

In his dream, a king thought he was a beggar. When he awoke, he saw the queen sleeping beside him and looked upon his servants and kingdom. He paused and wondered, Am I a king who was dreaming he was a beggar, or am I a beggar who is dreaming that he is a king? Upon reflection, the king realized that, in the final analysis, he is closer to being the beggar because, when he dies, he cannot take his kingdom with him. He will have to leave this world empty-handed. The king was awakened to the truth that only the spiritual reality is lasting. Worldly happiness comes and goes, but spiritual happiness is permanent. The soul is eternal, so when we connect with the soul, we gain everlasting happiness.

Connect the material life to spirituality to find meaning and happiness

Our lives are comprised of two parts: the material life and the spiritual life; body and soul. Each one affects the other, and the only time they separate is at death. To attain happiness in our physical and material lives, it is vital that we connect our material outlook to spirituality. For example, if we work with honesty and integrity with a view to supporting our family and contributing to society and those who are less fortunate than we are, our work becomes connected to spirituality. If we study hard to make the world a better place, our studying becomes connected to spirituality. If we nurture our children and provide them the ethics and principles to guide their decisions and the self-esteem to believe in themselves and their abilities, then our caring for our children is connected to spirituality. These are some ways in which we can translate our material actions to spirituality. Spirituality does not just exist in places of worship; it is right in our midst, in everything we do from dusk to dawn.

The spiritual journey leads us back to ourselves

Spirituality rests right within us, waiting to be recognized and explored. The journey to spiritual discovery is an arduous one. Pure and ethical living, meditation, prayer, and good deeds are some ingredients that develop our spirituality.

In the book, *The Conference of the Birds*, Farid-ud-din Attar talks about hundreds of birds who venture to meet the Supreme Being. The journey is difficult, and eventually most of the birds give up. Only thirty of them manage to complete the journey. When they reach the home of the Supreme Being, to their bewilderment they come face to face with a huge mirror. Seeing their own selves reflected in the mirror, they discover that the spirit has always rested inside each one of them. The essence of the story is that connecting with the spirit is a challenging task that is accomplished only when one has overcome the barriers of materialism and impurity and has become worthy of discovering the spirit that has always rested within.

This spiritual cleansing or purification is analogous to a mirror that is so coated with dust that it no longer gives a reflection. Once the dust is removed, the mirror shines and the reflection is crystal clear. Similarly, when the dust of material impurities is removed by pure and ethical living, service to humanity, nonviolence to self or others, and meditation, we come face to face with our spiritual essence.

Divine laws guide our actions and connections

We were all born of spirit. All of us, irrespective of creed, color, race, or religion, are interconnected and interdependent, guided by divine principles of truth and justice. We all laugh and cry in the same language. When we are hurt and cry, it is the language of pain; when we are happy and laugh, it is the language of joy. When we hurt others, we are hurting ourselves. This is the reciprocal law of divine nature.

One day while I was meditating, my then two-year-old son, Tawfiq, was disturbing me. I had three choices. I could get upset with Tawfiq, ignore him altogether, or hug him. I decided to stop meditating and hug Tawfiq. In so doing, I reaped a richer spiritual experience than I likely would have had meditating.

One day I parked my car in my garage and got out to pick up something from the trunk. I noticed that I had crushed a worm on the ground and that the worm was struggling in pain. I was sad seeing the worm hopelessly in pain, yet I tried to ignore the incident by saying to myself that it was only a worm and was not a big deal. Then a thought struck me: What if a giant crushed me and brushed aside my pain? How would I feel? At that moment I felt compassion for the worm. I could not do much to help the struggling worm except offer a small prayer beseeching relief. I felt, though, that my prayer reached the worm through some spiritual force. I cannot explain how this happened, but I am convinced that it did.

Spiritual connection lives on in our hearts

When we do things in life that touch people, those loving actions remain in these people's thoughts and hearts even after we die. My cousin Altaz wrote this poem upon the untimely death of my uncle Mohamed:

Your whole life was dedicated to bringing joy to others
And this you surely did, my dear uncle;
Leaving all of us memories so fond and so pure
That for this great loss we may never find a cure.
But it is said, "He, the Master, shall giveth life and when
it's time, He taketh away;
So, for the nourishment of the soul, through its journey
you must pray."
And all our prayers are with you every step of the way
Feeling your eternal presence each and every day.
May your soul rest and transcend to the level above
For no one brought more meaning to the greatest of words: Love.
May your kind and precious soul live in immense peace for
all eternity
And through our prayers reach the highest plateau –
the Oneness –
The Final State of Divinity.
Amen

At the beginning of this book, I wrote about knowing ourselves, and that true knowing entails connecting with our spirit, which is where the essence of our true self is revealed. This is not an easy process, and results will not come overnight; but, as we continue to live a pure, ethical, and spiritually devoted life, we will gradually connect with the spirit. Finally, when we connect with the spirit, we open the door to eternal happiness.

ASK YOURSELF:

Am I aware of my innate spiritual nature?

What am I doing to foster and develop it?

Am I connecting with other human beings on a spiritual level?

When innocent children suffer, does it matter whose children they are?

When I see another person, what do I see? Do I focus on his or her appearance, character, personality, or soul? Do I try to see the soul beyond his or her physical attributes?

Do I look for the spiritual meaning of the experiences I have in life?

HOW TO GET STARTED:

Make a commitment to undertake at least one regular spiritual practice in your daily life. Choose something you best relate to, be it meditation, prayer, or communion with nature.

The next time one of your colleagues is experiencing a trauma or dealing with a difficult situation, try to connect and empathize with that person and truly feel his or her pain and suffering.

Look deeper into a person than his or her appearance and personality. Being able to do this takes time. It requires us to remain nonjudgmental, keep an open mind, and take the time to see where the person is coming from.

Feel the Power
of Prayer

Prayer supported by faith can move mountains.

A Sufi saying

Prayer is an expression of Divine love and a communication between ourselves and the Creator. This dialogue can be with whichever Holy Being we believe in – Jesus, Ram, Buddha, the Earth, Allah, the Higher Being, or simply our inner spirit. Prayer is a supplication – an expression of gratitude and a humble request. The meaning of prayer is different for everyone.

Just as there is no one definition of prayer, there is no one way of praying. Everyone prays in the way he or she is most comfortable, as the following story illustrates. The Prophet Moses was walking through the fields when he came upon a shepherd who was deep in prayer. The shepherd was praying out loud and saying that if he were to meet God, he would offer Him a bowl of soup, wash His feet in milk, clean Him, and brush lice out of His hair. When Moses heard the shepherd praying in such a manner, he admonished him and told him that God is supreme and beyond all human conception. He asked the shepherd to recite the formal prayers. The shepherd was taken aback and deeply hurt. After this incident, Moses did not receive any communication from God for many days, and, when he finally did, he was told that his behavior toward the shepherd was unacceptable. God explained that the shepherd was praying in the best way he knew, which was perfectly fine – just as Moses's way of praying was the appropriate one for him.

This personal interpretation and expression of prayer does not diminish the merit of more formal and established prayers. These provide consistency and familiar reminders of the spiritual life. These types of prayers, such as the Lord's Prayer, have to be translated into action, however, if they are to be effective in dynamically connecting to the Divine.

Prayer strengthens faith and faith strengthens prayer

Prayer is intimately connected to faith. When we board an airplane, our faith in the pilot's ability to fly allows us to relax. Without that faith, we would not board the plane in the first place. Similarly, without faith we would probably not pray at all. When we have faith, our prayers are strengthened and can work wonders for us, which in turn strengthens our faith.

Susan's sister was suffering from cancer, so Susan went to visit her for a few days. When she got there, she found her sister's physical state deteriorating. Her sister was feeling hopeless and was counting her last days. She was also really concerned about the welfare of her two-year-old child. Susan and her family had faith and prayed intensely for her recovery. A few days later, not only was her sister physically feeling better, but her attitude had also changed significantly. Susan says that she experienced the power of her and her family's faith in the fruition of their prayers.

Prayers are said for many reasons

World leaders and athletes have said prayers at important and critical moments. Similarly, people in difficulty and stress have resorted to prayers. Some say prayers to carry them through the day, and others to fulfill their missions and aspirations in life. It is okay to pray in this manner. However, one of the finest prayers is to say thank you for all we already have. When we appreciate and express our thanks for whatever we have, we create further abundance and growth.

Prayer paves the way to spiritual development

Prayer is a powerful vehicle for spiritual connection; it gives us strength, solace, comfort, and courage, and clears the path for our spiritual development. None of us are perfect; we all make mistakes. Our shortcomings present obstacles in our spiritual path. One way of paving the way to our spiritual illumination and awakening is through daily prayer. All prayers are good; it is better to say any prayer than not to pray at all. However, prayer that addresses our frailties and spurs us to action is the most effective. Daily prayer is a reminder of what our aspirations are and to continue to strive toward our spiritual mission.

ASK YOURSELF:

Is there something that I should be thankful for?

Have I done something wrong or hurt someone today or in the past?

Do I need strength to accomplish something that I am unable to carry out or get going?

Have I tried a daily prayer to help me accomplish the above?

HOW TO GET STARTED:

Get started with any prayer, no matter how short. Start each day with a short prayer seeking guidance, and end each day with a prayer of gratitude.

On the following page is the daily prayer that I say. It helps me connect with my mission because what I seek in my daily prayer is to live in alignment with my mission. It also inspires me to go out and give one hundred percent to my day. This is only one way of praying – there are many other ways. Your prayer will evolve as time goes by; mine is constantly evolving. I recite this prayer every morning and evening (usually with my family) to get help from God to realize my aspirations.

God, thank You for all You have given us: good health, a loving family, peace, basic necessities, dignity, education, the capacity and wisdom to serve, friends, livelihood, and countless other gifts. We are grateful for Your kindness.

O God, You are all-forgiving; please forgive our trespassing. Those who may have trespassed against us, we forgive them wholeheartedly.

Give us the strength to be kind, virtuous, pious, modest, truthful, patient, tolerant, and enduring. Give us the strength never to be haughty, jealous, lustful, greedy, angry, or judgmental.

Give us the strength to make the right decisions when it comes to our family, profession, finances, attendance at prayers, business, contributions to others, and relationships.

Give food, clothing, shelter, peace, and success to those who are poor, needy, sick, weak, or old . Eliminate their difficulties and give them strength, courage, and inner happiness. Give us the strength to help them in all the ways we can.

Give us the strength to inspire our daughter, Sahar, and our son, Tawfiq, to strive for excellence, actualize their fullest potential, and contribute to humankind, and help us to be true role models to them. Help us to give them the roots – the principles and ethics by which they will make decisions in life – and wings – the self-esteem with which they will aim high and not succumb to temptation. Give us the strength to inspire in a similar manner all children with whom we come in contact. Give us the strength to inspire ourselves in a similar manner.

Give us the strength to live with integrity, make a positive difference in the lives of others, enjoy the process of life, and remember that whatever success we have, is through Your grace, and we are just instruments carrying out Your wishes. Amen.

Practice Meditation

Even a good thing is not as good as nothing.

Zen phrase

Meditation means different things to different people. In its basic form, meditation means sitting quietly, doing nothing, and being empty of all thought. It is a practice that relaxes and stills the mind of the endless chatter and clutter of our multitudinous thoughts. Meditation is a vehicle that allows us to contact our deepest spiritual core or center which is the essence of our being.

There are different variations of how meditation is done, but the essence is the same. Traditional methods of meditation have rules and methods, whereas the modern schools promote an open-ended style of meditation. The form may vary, but the ultimate goal remains the same. The objective is to attempt to tap into the Divine Reality and draw strength from it. Yoga, transcendental meditation, Hindu jaap, Buddhist mantra, or the Sufi word are some of the different schools of meditation.

The key to inner peace and happiness lies within us

Meditation takes us on a journey inside ourselves to seek a connection with the Divine essence. This practice, if sufficiently strong and dedicated, has the potential to bring about spiritual enlightenment, which arises when we understand the deeper mystery and meaning of life. The road to enlightenment has many levels and stages, and involves stripping away layers of illusion and delusion to get to the underlying spiritual truth – the heart of Divine realization.

The key to happiness and inner peace is inside us and not outside. Meditation helps us find that key. Nasruddin, a mystic, spoke of a man who had lost his keys and was looking for them in the street. A friend joined him in looking for the keys, but they were unsuccessful. The friend then asked the man exactly where he had lost his keys, to which the man replied that he had lost them at home. When asked why he was looking for the keys out in the street, his simple reply was that there was more light in the street. The symbolic meaning here is that we are looking for the key to the spirit in bright places, but not the right place, which is within us. Meditation connects us to this place of illumination inside ourselves, even if it means going into some dark places along the way.

When we meditate in absolute humility, we progress on the spiritual journey. When a saint, through her devout meditation, reached the highest state of enlightenment, a voice asked, "Who are you?"

The saint replied, "It is me."

The voice responded, "Out you go."

The saint continued her meditation and again came very close to the Reality. Again the voice said, "Who are you?"

This time she replied, "It is your servant."

The voice again said, "Out you go."

Once more the saint continued with her meditation until she attained the highest state of consciousness. The voice once more said, "Who are you?" Now she replied, "It is you," and was finally let in to experience the Reality. The moral of this Sufi story is that we become something when we become nothing. When we eliminate our ego, we experience enlightenment. You and I become one. I and you become one.

Meditation helps us cope and transforms our experience

In this modern era, we live at a frantic pace. There is so much going on and so much to attend to that our minds are crowded with many details that can scatter themselves into chaos until we experience the stress of overload. Meditation on this roller-coaster ride of life is truly a lifesaver, a breath of fresh air. Meditation calms us down, neutralizes stress, and helps us gain balance, stability, and a fresh outlook. To be most effective, meditation should be carried out at a time and place of least disturbance. This allows us to really let go of worldly pressures.

Meditation builds character, lends determination, and develops concentration skills. I started meditating regularly at 4:00 a.m. in 1972 because I felt a need to embark on a spiritual quest. This was a turning point in my life. From being a lazy, undirected young man, I turned into a serious, intelligent student. I also began to see life in a different manner – one that has a deeper purpose and meaning. My regular practice of meditation was instrumental in bringing about a personal transformation.

Concentration and discipline are important ingredients of meditation

While meditating, it is important to rid ourselves of worldly thoughts and to concentrate on spiritual thought – the word, mantra, divine energy, light, love, nature, or the divine essence of life. There is a Sufi story where the great Shibli went to visit the illustrious master, Thauri. The master was sitting so still that not a hair moved. Shibli asked, "Where did you learn such stillness?" Thauri replied, "From a cat. He was watching a mouse hole with even greater concentration than you have seen in me!"

There is a cost to everything in life. When we gain something, we give up something else. It is a question of choice. If we desire inner happiness and peace, we will forgo other activities to find the time to meditate. With regular practice, this discipline can develop into a powerful habit that helps us to cope, stay centered, and make sense of our daily lives.

ASK YOURSELF:

What is the deeper meaning of life?

Where can I find the key to my inner happiness?

How can I connect with the soul?

HOW TO GET STARTED:

Find a quiet time and space to recite a symbolic word or mantra. This could be the name of God, nature, or a multitude of other words relating to divine energy. Alternatively, contemplate nature – think of the ocean, a bird flying, rain drops falling from the sky, a calm lake, or a mountain.

Try meditating at dawn; it is a powerful way of awakening the deeper consciousness.

Simply sit quietly and focus on your breath rising and falling.

Reflect on and Appreciate Nature

*The leaves of the green trees for the one who
contemplates are like pages of a book. Every page is like a book
about the gnosis of the Creator.*

Sa'adi

hen we are attuned with nature, we are in harmony
with our surroundings. As we feel the oneness with
everything around us, we subtly become gentler, kinder,
and more loving to everyone – including ourselves. This tenderness
relaxes us and gives us a calmer disposition which greatly contributes to
our well-being and overall happiness. Some therapists recognize the especially soothing effect of nature and may meet with their clients in the
woods or other natural settings that provide the right ambience for healing to take place.

Nature has many lessons to teach us

When we contemplate how nature works, we get a glimpse of the
wonder of creation. We begin to understand the beauty and wisdom of the
universe. For example, bees build houses one beside the other in perfect
shapes and harmony, and ants build complete and complex dwellings
underground. It is phenomenal to see how the entire Universe and
creation works. The following example further illustrates this point.

One cold and windy day, my cousin, Salim, was waiting for a bus
to get to a doctor's appointment. He was running late, and the bus seemed
to take forever to come. Salim was losing his cool and fretting and fuming.
Suddenly, his eyes lit on a tall tree bending down gently with the pressure

and force of the wind. The tree seemed to be telling him that the best way to go through a stormy day is to bend down and give in to it. He reflected on this message and realized that his wisest action in this situation over which he had no control was simply to let go and surrender. With this realization, he was able to let go of his frustrations and relax.

Witness the effortless activities and growth in nature. The trees do not resist the winds, the blade of grass grows steadily, and the birds fly seemingly without effort. If we reflect on nature's activities, we gain the valuable insight that there is no need to push the river – that the natural and easy way is simply to go with the flow and let ourselves surrender to the moment in the great river of life.

Nature reveals the secret wisdom of creation

The cycle of the seasons shows us that creation is perpetually evolving, that after every freezing winter there is a warm and golden summer. Similarly, in the cycle of our lives, we need not despair in troubled times. The cycle of the seasons can also be compared to the span of a human life. Our birth or childhood is like spring, youth like summer, middle age like autumn, and old age or death, like winter. These seasons of life are cyclical and short, and after every death, life is reborn. Life is the beginning of death, and death the beginning of life. Contemplating nature is akin to prayer and meditation, as nature reveals the secret wisdom of the universe.

Our contemplation of nature reveals the true meaning of life, and as we get in tune, balance, and harmony with our glorious earth, we become happy inhabitants of it.

ASK YOURSELF:

What messages do I derive from nature?

When was the last time I saw a sunrise or sunset and reflected on the colors and shadows?

When was the last time I looked at myself or another person and marveled at what wonderful creations we are?

Have I noticed how the birds fly or the ducks swim and appreciated the wonder of life?

HOW TO GET STARTED:

Try to feel nature as part of your own being and ever present in your life. Experience becoming one with nature by going for a walk in a forest, swimming in the ocean, or watching a mountaintop from an airplane.

Try to become the sun for a few minutes. Imagine yourself giving light to the entire universe and reflect on the role that you are playing.

Imagine what it would be like to become:

A bird soaring freely in the skies

The rain pouring from the skies to the ground

The wind blowing gently

The moon lighting the night

Another human

Experience the feeling, the oneness with nature in each of these examples. There is no one single way to practice this. You need only to find some quiet time and scenic environment where you can sit in contemplation. It will be difficult to connect at first; however, with time and practice, it will get easier.

Draw Meaning from Suffering

*Your pain is the breaking of the shell
that encloses your understanding.*

Kahlil Gibran

Earlier, in the section "Maintain Positive Attitudes," I wrote about turning sorrow and suffering into opportunity. Now this is not always possible. However, when we are unable to turn our tragedy into opportunity, we can either suffer more by focusing on the negative consequences, or try to make some meaning out of suffering to soften our pain.

I do not want to dismiss suffering in any way because I know how horrific and unfathomable it can be. I saw my grandmother paralyzed and unable to move for a long time before her death. A good friend of mine became totally incapacitated in her twenties. I witnessed a client pass away in his forties, leaving behind two toddlers. When I went to Pakistan to work with Afghan refugees, I saw children whose parents had been killed in front of their eyes. In my travels to India and Pakistan, I saw countless children sleeping in the streets with nothing more than begging to look forward to the next day. I am making a case for trying to look at suffering in a different light, finding some deeper meaning in it, and, in the process, bringing understanding and easing some pain.

Sorrow and joy are inseparable

The paradox of life is that joy and tragedy go hand in hand; we need one to appreciate the other. The deeper our sorrow, the deeper our joy. Sorrow is a great teacher and companion. To ask for joy without sorrow is like asking for tea without leaves. If winter is here, can spring be far away? If night is here, can day be far away? If hardship is here, can joy be far away? The answer is no. When the night is at its darkest, dawn is close by. And only when we know and accept darkness, can we recognize the light.

Suffering brings us closer to one another

When we grieve in others' sorrows, we forget our own. Through suffering, we learn to empathize with others going through similar pain. Suffering can sometimes bring about an occasion to help. It can create opportunities for human beings to help one another. It brings people together. When my grandmother died in 1992, our whole family came from across the globe to pay their final respects. We all bonded in this grieving.

Suffering can lead to inner richness

Suffering gives us a better understanding of who we are. It forces us to look inward, and this inner quest enriches us. The Sufi Rumi says, "I lost everything I had, but in the process I found myself."

We too often judge suffering from the outside, instead of from the inside. Consider Helen Keller, who was incapable of hearing and seeing for almost all her life yet, before she died, revealed that her life had been very fulfilling. Napoleon Bonaparte on the other hand, had everything – yet before he died he said, " I have not seen six happy days in my life."

Suffering brings about humility – too much unbridled success can lead to pride or "the pride that goeth before the fall." Kahlil Gibran says, "The flute that soothes your spirit is the very wood that is hallowed with knives." The wood had to be chopped before producing the beautiful sound.

Suffering carries deeper meaning

Incidents in life are not always as they may appear to be on the surface. If we explore closely, they often have a deeper meaning. There was once a wise old man who was visited by his disciple. The disciple wanted to gain a deeper understanding of why things happen in life. The sage told the disciple that he was not ready to learn from him. However, since the disciple would not take "no" for an answer, the wise man eventually agreed to teach him.

The old man showed the disciple a father making a dent in his child's cart, an old uncle hiding his grandchildren's treasure left behind by their late parents, and a young child being killed in an accident. The wise old man asked the disciple what meaning he made of all these occurrences.

The disciple said that the father was a mad man to make a dent in his child's cart because the child needed the cart to make a living for the family. As for the old uncle, the disciple said he was a greedy man taking away the children's rightful treasure left to them by their loving parents. For the child's death, the disciple blamed the Higher Being for having no compassion for the child's next of kin.

The sage responded by saying that if the disciple wanted to know the deeper meaning of things, he must understand the following interpretations: The father made a dent in the cart to save the cart from being taken for war by the king's men. The old uncle hid the treasure to save it for the children when they came of age and to prevent their step aunt from misusing the treasure. And as for the child killed in the accident, the sage explained that it was to interfere with the child's destiny as a murderer. The disciple was confounded by these interpretations. The old wise man told him to come back next year when he was ready to learn. Suffering makes us ponder the mysteries of life. Life is a mystery to live in – not to solve. That point hits home when we are unable to demystify the suffering.

Suffering carries within it a hidden good

For every bad happening, there is a good one hidden somewhere – if we look for it. A man was walking near the beach and contemplating the beauty around him. He got so carried away in his reverie that he walked for many miles and became lost. He was tired and cold and sad. In the midst of finding his path back home, he came across an alluring stone, which he picked up and put in his pocket. Years later, the man lost his job and reached rock bottom when he had no money left. In desperation, he took the stone to a jeweler to see if it had any value. The jeweler appraised the stone and announced its value was six times the man's annual salary. If the man had not lost his way on the beach, he would not have found the stone. Furthermore, if he had not lost his job, he would have never known the value of the stone.

Suffering can extend capacity and amplify hidden gifts. As Richard Bach says, "There is no such thing as a problem without a gift for you in its hands. You seek problems because you need their gifts."

Suffering is a design to make our lives meaningful and give us something to aspire to. If we have everything we want in life, the challenge of life goes away and can lead to boredom and stagnation. The following adaptation of Shel Silverstein's adult fairy tale illustrates this.

There was once a circle that felt terribly dejected because it was missing a piece. So the circle started on a journey looking for the missing piece. Now, because it had a piece missing, it could only roll slowly as it ventured in search of the missing piece. On route, the circle chatted with a butterfly, smelled some roses, admired the sunrise and sunset, tried on different pieces, and chatted with everyone it met. Even so, the circle was feeling low because none of the pieces it tried on was the missing piece. Finally, it found a piece that fit exactly. Now the circle was complete and could roll easily and swiftly.

After a few days, however, the circle was sad again because it was traveling so fast it had no time to chat with the butterfly, smell the roses, admire the sunrise and sunset, and chat with other pieces. So it decided to remove another piece of itself and go on another journey looking for that missing piece. In a way, we all are like the circle with a missing piece. Our inadequacies are part of the design of our lives that gives them meaning and purpose.

ASK YOURSELF:

Can you remember a time when you suffered deeply or felt great sorrow? What meaning or lesson did you learn from that particular sorrow?

Can you think of something good that came out of a misfortune in your life?

Can you think of an instance where another's suffering brought you closer to him or her?

Have there been times when suffering has been instrumental in your life and development?

HOW TO GET STARTED:

Make a list of recent misfortunes you have faced.

Try comparing these to the sorrow and suffering faced by people in the war-torn and poverty-stricken places of the world.

Reflect on what positive things came from these misfortunes. These positives may not be apparent, but, when we look deep within ourselves, we will find them.

AWAKEN YOUR SPIRITUALITY

Our spirituality is awakened through prayers, meditation, pure intentions, forgiveness, ethical living, and connecting our daily lives to spirituality.

In this section we have covered the following key points:

- The physical body is temporary, but the spirit is eternal.

- Balance between our spiritual lives and material lives is a key to happiness.

- We connect with the spirit when we translate our daily actions and behavior into spirituality.

- Prayers are a powerful medium of healing, hope, and faith.

- Meditation is a higher form of concentration and not only relieves stress but connects us to the deep meaning of life.

- Nature has many lessons to teach us. By contemplating nature we can potentially become attuned to our surroundings.

- Ethical living is the way to marry our material and spiritual lives.

- Our pure intentions are the roots that give rise to persistence, success, and happiness.

- When we forgive wholeheartedly, we unleash our creative energies.

- Suffering is an integral part and parcel of life. We all have our share of suffering, some more and some less. Upon reflection, we can find deep meaning in suffering. For every bad thing that happens, there is some good.

7

ENJOY
THE
RIDE

*Yesterday is history,
Tomorrow is a mystery,
Today is a gift, that is
why it is called the present.
Seize the moment! Carpe Diem!*
                    Anonymous

This section will address the following questions:

How long is our life?

•

Why is the moment "now" so precious?

•

What happens when we postpone happiness?

Savor the Moment

Happy the man, and happy he alone
He who can call today his own
He who, secure within, can say,
Tomorrow, do thy worst,
For I have liv'd today.

John Dryden

e are always postponing living: when I finish writing my book, when my children grow up, when I retire, when I move out, when I get married. The time for living is now; if we are not happy now, when will we ever be happy? Every moment is a priceless blessing. Happiness is not a destination, it is a process. Life is a journey to be savored every step of the way. As Abraham Lincoln said, "People are as happy as they make up their minds to be."

Live in the moment with no regrets

Our journey through life is short, like the blinking of the eyes, a brief journey through eternity. Our birth or childhood is like dawn, youth like noon, middle age like evening, and death like midnight. We cannot live forever. No one knows when his or her time or that of his or her loved ones will be up. If we leave things for tomorrow, we may risk never doing them, and we may never get to share with people in the ways we truly desire.

The Indian poet Kabir said, *"Kal kare so aaj; aaj kare so abb,"* or, "Whatever we plan to do tomorrow, we should do today; whatever we plan to do today, we should do right now." There is no better moment than right now – especially when it comes to the important things in life like spending time with our families and our close ones and for spiritual endeavors such as meditating and serving humanity.

I always used to postpone living. I was so engrossed in excelling and striving that I had no time or patience for my loved ones. When I contemplated the time it would take for me to achieve what I wanted, I realized that my kids would be grown up and I would have missed their childhood. I also realized that whatever I wanted to do then, I could probably do now – so why postpone it?

Living in the present moment means being spontaneous and going with the rhythm of each new day. It means not resisting things around us, accepting things as they are, and not always wishing things were different. The tree does not resist the wind, but bends to let the wind through. Similarly, when we take each of life's challenges as just a temporary obstacle, then we will find the journey of life to be smooth and enjoyable.

Living in the present enables us to focus our energies and skills on the current situation

When we live in the present, we are able to capitalize on the opportunities of the moment. Often, we carry the baggage of the past or the worry of the future and let our precious energy slip away. I used to live with a lot of past baggage and was seldom relaxed. Then I started noticing my son, Tawfiq, capturing life to the fullest without a care in the world. In watching Tawfiq, I got my first taste of realizing what it would be like to live fully in the moment, and this is something I now strive toward daily.

Our past baggage – the past hurts, losses, and umpteen other things – is gone, and gone forever. And our future is only unfolding with each moment; there is no other future. By starting afresh in each moment, our energy is fully channeled into our current endeavors and toward our immediate happiness.

I once read a thought-provoking analogy which to the best of my knowledge is anonymous. Imagine there is a bank that credits your account every morning with $86,400, carries over no balance from day to day, allows you to keep no cash balance, and every evening cancels whatever part of the amount you have failed to use during the day. What would you do? Draw out every cent of course! Well, everyone has such a bank. It is called TIME. Every morning, it credits you with 86,400 seconds. Every night it writes off, as lost, whatever of this you have failed to invest to good purpose, and carries over no balance. It allows no over-draft. Each day it opens a new account for you. Each night it burns the records of the day. If you fail to use the day's deposits, the loss is yours. There is no going back. There is no drawing against the "tomorrow."

As we live every day as if it was our last day and do good to others, our life expands and flourishes. Every day becomes like eternity, every minute precious and enjoyable. Life is the art of drawing without an eraser – give it your best in the moment and let it be a masterpiece.

ASK YOURSELF:

Am I carrying the baggage of the past or the fear of the future?

How do I bring about harmony between living spontaneously and seizing every moment versus the need for planning and creating a road map for the future?

If I owned the whole world: How many meals a day could I eat? How many houses could I live in? How many cars could I drive? How many beds could I sleep in? How much do we really need?

Do I postpone my living and happiness to the future? Why?

HOW TO GET STARTED:

Watch a clock for one minute. Watch the 60 seconds go by. See how long it takes. Experience how time expands when we are present.

Take an hour to live fully in the present. In that hour, do something that gives happiness to you and your loved ones. To accomplish this, you may want to pretend that this is the last hour of your life. Imagine you are called by the Angel of Death to leave this world in an hour. What would you do?

Notice how focused you feel and how your energies are channeled to this one end. Try taking one hour a day to begin with and practice the art of focus, concentration, and living in the moment.

Do not forget to be happy now. In the middle of an argument or a lousy day, take a washroom break or go for a walk around the block. During the break try putting things into perspective, and remind yourself that what you are fretting about is not a big deal.

Remind yourself daily that most of us have everything we need to be happy. If we are not happy with whatever little we have, we will probably not be happier with more possessions.

ENJOY THE RIDE

As we work on the previous six steps to achieving lasting happiness, we should not forget that happiness is now, in this very moment. That is the seventh step. Sustained happiness is earned by working on the six steps; however, perpetual happiness comes from enjoying the effort and the ride through the journey of life.

In this section we have covered the following key points:

- Every day is a giving opportunity.

- Life is short. Live it. Give it. Enjoy it.

- Yesterday is gone, and tomorrow may never be. Today is a blessing. Cherish it.

- Life is the art of drawing without an eraser. Let ours be a happy masterpiece.

- Happiness is not in a far-off land. It is here and now.

REVISITING THE SEVEN STEPS

Step One

Discover Yourself

There is a purpose in each of our lives. We may need to dig deep within ourselves to find out what that purpose is, but the clearer our mission is, the better are our chances of accomplishing it.

Each day is a new day, a day that brings fresh learning about ourselves and our environment. For this learning to happen, we need to be alert and reflect on our experiences. We are bound to learn at least one powerful lesson daily if we are fully conscious of what is going on around us.

Every choice we make shapes our destiny. Therefore, let us make wise choices that are consistent with the type of destiny we are aspiring to.

Step Two

Maintain Positive Attitudes

We are all gifted and blessed in our own unique ways. When we treasure who we are and believe in our inherent capabilities, we find that the world also starts to believe in us. When we are willing to bet on ourselves, the world will bet on us as well.

A blessing comes our way daily. Some people may appear to receive more blessings than others. However, the more we focus on what we have and what we are receiving daily, the more blessings we attract. So counting our blessings not only makes us focus on the positive things in our lives but also creates the energy for multiplication of these blessings.

We have no control over what others think and do. The only control we have is over our thoughts and actions. The more we concentrate on our thoughts and capacity, the more we take control of our happiness. This means ceasing to worry about what others think and giving people the benefit of the doubt.

The most we can be expected to do is our best. It is a good feeling when we win in the race of life, but it is an even better feeling when we know that we have done our best – irrespective of winning or losing. Once we have used all our faculties and given our best, we cease to worry about the rest; whatever happens subsequently happens for the best.

In the journey of life there will be highs as well as lows. This is the law of nature. We need to be as happy during our lows as we are during our highs, because every low comes in a package with a beautiful lesson. When we go about our lives with confidence and poise, we gain respect. When we become egoistic, we become shallow and lose respect.

Step Three
Hone Your Life Skills

We have multiple roles to play in life and only a finite amount of time to meet all our responsibilities and to realize our aspirations. Our focus on key priorities and a balanced outlook enable us to get through the maze of responsibilities and achieve harmony and success.

When we work with pride, empower others, and become true leaders in every walk of life, we begin to make a positive difference in our lives and in those of others around us.

Step Four
Build Healthy Relationships

Our relationships with our close ones play a big part in our lives. When we have healthy relationships filled with love, respect, dialogue, and learning, we experience abounding happiness.

Step Five
Let Ethics and Values Be Your Guide

Ethical living, forgiveness, and pure intentions enable us to connect with the spirit, thereby tuning into divinity and bliss.

Of all the joys that there may be, the joy of giving is one of the best. When we bring true joy to the lives of others, we create joy in our own lives. The more we give, the more we have.

Step Six
Awaken Your Spirituality

Unlike our physical existence, our spiritual lives are eternal. If we want lasting happiness, then we need to live a spiritual life. This can be done by connecting our physical actions to spirituality. Whatever we do, we should assess its spiritual merit. By doing so, we can transform our physical acts into spiritual ones.

With daily prayers, meditation, contemplation of nature, and connection with the spirit, we can turn our lives into blissful living.

Step Seven
Enjoy the Ride

Happiness is a choice we can all make. So let us make that choice and begin to be happy now. Happiness is not in a distant land but right here in our midst. As we think happy and are happy, we are able to face life's challenges with confidence and relative ease. Working on the first six steps in this book gives us internal contentment of having lived to our full potential and living an ethical and empowering life, but it is the seventh step that brings about the fun and joy of life. The seventh step without the first six can bring about limited happiness, but lasting and sustained happiness comes from working on the first six steps whilst savoring and enjoying the process.

Afterward

If we have done all the exercises in the book, we should be on our way to self discovery – knowing our strengths and weaknesses, changing our attitudes, developing our life skills, building our relationships, awakening our spirituality, and enjoying happiness. The principles in my book are not easy to implement and internalize. I must admit that I struggle with some of them on a daily basis. The idea is not to master them all overnight, but rather to be aware of them and gradually practice and internalize them so as to find lasting happiness. Once you have internalized all the principles, give this book to a friend. Until then, keep it by your bedside.

My best wishes go to all of you. May you find inner happiness and deep meaning in your lives, reach your fullest potential, and make a positive difference in the lives of others.

Suggested Reading

Bach, Richard. *Illusions.* Great Britain: William Heinemann, 1977

Brunton, Dr. Paul. *Discover Yourself.* York Beach, Maine: E.P. Dutton & Co., 1939

Buscaglia, Leo. *Living, Loving and Learning.* New York: Fawcett Columbine, 1982

Carlson, Richard. *Don't Sweat the Small Stuff.... and it's all small stuff.* New York: Hyperion, 1977

Carnegie, Dale. *How To Stop Worrying and Start Living.* New York: Pocket Books, 1984

Caufield, Jack and Mark Victor Hansen. *Chicken Soup for the Soul* Deerfield Beach, FL: Health Communications, 1993

Chopra, Deepak. *The Seven Spiritual Laws of Success.* California: San Rafael, 1994

Covey, Stephen R. *First Things First.* New York: Simon & Schuster, 1994

Covey, Stephen R. *The 7 Habits of Highly Effective People.* New York: Simon & Schuster, 1989

De Angelis, Barbara. *Real Moments.* New York: Dell Publishing, 1994

Dyer, Wayne W. *Manifest Your Destiny.* New York: Harper Collins, 1997

Friedlandera, Shams. *When You Hear Hoofbeats, Think of a Zebra.* California: Mazda, 1987

Gibran, Kahlil. *The Prophet.* New York: Alfred A. Knopf, 1923

Goleman, Daniel. *Emotional Intelligence.* New York: Bantam Books, 1995

Gray, John. *Men Are From Mars and Women Are From Venus.* New York: Harper Collins, 1992

Heider, John. *The Tao of Leadership.* Atlanta: Humanics New Age, 1985

Hendriks, Gay and Kate Ludeman. *The Corporate Mystic.* New York: Bantam Books, 1996

Hill, Napoleon. *Think and Grow Rich.* New York: Fawcett Crest, 1983

Jansen, Jo Ann. *Define Yourself and Discover Your Destiny!* British Columbia, 1995

Kehoe, John. *The Practice of Happiness.* British Columbia: Zoetic Inc., 1999

Khamisa, Azim. *Azim's Bardo.* California: Rising Star Press, 1998

Mandino, Og. *The Greatest Salesman in the World.* New York, 1968

Mayer, Jeffrey. *If You Haven't Got the Time to Do It Right, When Will You Find the Time to Do It Over?* New York: Simon & Schuster, 1990

Schwartz, David J. *The Magic of Thinking Big.* New York: Simon & Schuster, 1987

Shah, Idries. *The Sufis.* New York: Doubleday & Company, 1964

Sharma, Robin S. *The Monk Who Sold His Ferrari.* Ontario: Harper Collins, 1997

Whinefield, E.H. *Mathnavi I Ma'navi. The Spiritual Couplets of Rumi.* London: Octagon Press, 1979

Zukav, Gary. *The Seat of the Soul.* New York: Simon & Schuster, 1990

ORDER FORM

Seven Steps to Lasting Happiness

UNITED STATES	CANADA
_____ Copies @ $11.95 $ _____	_____ Copies @ $15.95 $ _____
GST (7%) $ _____	GST (7%) $ _____
Shipping (1st book) $ 4.00	Shipping (1st book) $ 4.00
Add $3.00 for each additional book $ _____	Add $3.00 for each additional book $ _____
Total enclosed $ _____	Total enclosed $ _____

PAYMENT: Make check or money order payable to:

Azim Jamal

10151 Gilmore Cresent, Ricmond, BC.

V6X 1X1

E-Mail: azim@azimjamal.com

Tel: (604) 733-0737 Fax: (604) 736-7511

For payment by credit card: ☐ MasterCard   ☐ Visa

Credit Card Account #_____

Expiry Date _____

Cardholder's Signature: _____

Ship to:

Name:_____

Address: (No PO Boxes please) _____

_____

_____

City/State and Zip/Postal Code: _____

Phone (work) _____ (home) _____

Thank you for your order!

Share your experiences of this book

If you have any comments about this book or any real-life stories you'd like to share, please write to me at:

E-Mail: azim@azimjamal.com

or mail at:
Azim Jamal
10151 Gilmore Crescent
Richmond, BC V6X 1X1
Canada

Visit my website at:
www.azimjamal.com